wine & food

wine & food

perfect pairings every time

Jane Parkinson

photography by **Toby Scott**

RYLAND PETERS & SMALL
LONDON • NEW YORK

Designers Manisha Patel and Paul Stradling
Commissioning Editor Stephanie Milner
Head of Production Patricia Harrington
Art Director Leslie Harrington
Editorial Director Julia Charles
Publisher Cindy Richards

Photographer Toby Scott
Photographer's Assistant Benjamin Wisely
Prop Stylist Luis Peral
Food Stylist Rosie Reynolds
Indexer Angie Hipkin

This edition published in 2017
First published in 2014
by Ryland Peters & Small,
20–21 Jockey's Fields,
London WC1R 4BW
and
341 E 116th St
New York NY 10029
www.rylandpeters.com

10 9 8 7 6 5 4 3 2 1

Printed and bound in China

ISBN: 978-1-84975-825-3

A CIP record for this book is available from the British
Library.

US Library of Congress cataloging-in-publication data
has been applied for.

contents

6	introduction	96	muscat
9	setting the wine scene	100	riesling
11	*A bit of label logic*	104	pinot grigio/pinot gris
		108	italian whites
12	**the bar**	110	spanish whites
14	temperature	114	**PICK THE RIGHT WINE:**
16	wine props		**FORTIFIED, SWEET & FIZZ**
18	glassware	116	fortified
21	*Same wine, different glass*	121	*Sherry*
		122	sweet
22	**the cellar**	126	fizz
24	**PICK THE RIGHT WINE: RED & ROSÉ**		
26	pinot noir	130	**the table**
31	*Chilling red wine*	132	meat
32	syrah/shiraz	139	*Surf 'n' turf*
36	cabernet sauvignon	140	fish & shellfish
41	*Let's talk tannin…*	146	veg
42	merlot	152	sauce
46	grenache & friends	155	*Store-cupboard wine matches*
50	spanish reds	156	spice
54	italian reds	161	*Time for takeout*
58	malbec	162	cheese
62	flagship reds		
66	rosé	172	resources
70	**PICK THE RIGHT WINE: WHITE**	172	index
72	viognier	176	acknowledgments
76	chardonnay		
81	*Organic, biodynamic, natural*		
82	sauvignon blanc		
87	*Party wines*		
88	chenin blanc		
92	semillon		

introduction

Feeling thirsty and hungry? Then this is the book for you. Seeing as I'm always asked what wines to drink, which are my favourites, and how to pair wine with food, I've decided to write it all down here as a go-to guide, for people who love all the flavours that come with wine, and wine with food. And so, I've written this book as though I'm talking to those people I chat to; you, my friends. It's about wine, sure, but it's about wine in my kind of everyday language, which means there's no room for jargon or geeky wine terms, unless I'm explaining what they mean, of course.

The way we buy, serve, enjoy and match wine has changed massively in the last decade or so, partly because we've never been so spoilt for choice. And with that in mind, in The Cellar, I introduce you to grape varieties, chatting about where each is grown and why it's made into wine there. I also discuss how wine should taste, why it tastes good, why it tastes bad, why it's notorious, why it's underrated or why it's blended with another grape. Friends also (always, always!) request recommendations of specific producers, the people who make the wine, so I've scattered quite a few of these throughout the book too, which I hope is useful for you.

In The Bar, I take a closer look at serving wine, whether it's the trends in glasses, nifty pieces of wine paraphernalia or looking at the temperature of a wine before drinking it. These things might all seem a bit old-school to some people, but they still play their part in delivering the ultimate wine experience.

While in The Table, you'll find some epic, traditional and quirky wine and food matches. It's organized by protein, mostly, but it was also important to add in a section on sauces, because so many of the dishes we eat today have their flavour dictated by the plate's so-called sideshow. There's also a dedicated spice section, because historically this is one of the most

unknown areas when it comes to wine and food matching. Naturally, I haven't been able to include every single sauce, spice or recipe, but there should be enough information inside about standout flavours to guide you to the right bottle for your dish.

This book is also peppered with pages that answer all sorts of ad hoc wine issues, and this is especially important for me, because I remember wishing somebody had answered these when I first got into wine. Within these, I take on everything from debunking the classic urban wine myths that just won't die, like how you can serve red wine with fish and why not all Sherry is sweet, but there are also pieces on the difference between natural and organic wine, the best wines to serve at parties or what to drink with ham and mustard, takeaway pizza or even fried chicken.

Also, at the bottom of this page you will see a bunch of symbols, all indicating a particular point of interest within the book, so when you spot one, just check back to this page to see what it's all about.

So, if you're interested in flavour, culture, language or travel, you don't need to be a nerd or have a fat wallet to understand or enjoy wine and food. And that's what this book is all about, so I hope you enjoy reading it. Cheers!

---

symbols used throughout this book

🏠 a grape's home region

👁 one to watch

★ a personal favourite

🏆 premium classification

⚡ wildcard

setting the wine scene

Knowing the name of the grape inside a bottle has completely changed the face of wine and how we drink it. Before my time, and possibly yours, too, wine names like Chablis, Bordeaux, Sancerre, Rioja and Chianti were flung about with such pomposity it gave wine completely the wrong image. That was turned on its head about 25–30 years ago, largely by people in the southern hemisphere and North America; places we call the New World. These guys started to make serious wine and had the confidence to slap the grape variety on the front of a bottle. This change to labelling wine opened the floodgates for wine appreciation, and instead of being something all highfalutin, wine became exciting, aspirational and easier to understand. Fast-track to today, and now there's just as much (if not more) global interest in the names Chardonnay, Cabernet Sauvignon, Merlot, Sauvignon Blanc, Tempranillo, or even Sangiovese, as there ever was in the Old World names of the regions in which these grape varieties were, and still are, made.

The new Old World

It's great news for us that countries like Italy, Spain, France and Portugal have raised their game in the face of stiff competition from New World winemakers. These countries are blessed with high-quality local grape varieties, each suited to its own special environment; and together with a general improvement in technology the world over, this now means there are tons of delicious European wines.

FRANCE

Whites

If you like that northern French, steely, grassy cut of Sauvignon Blanc without the posh-name price tag, try Sauvignon de Touraine from the Loire – the region that's home to those pricier names Pouilly-Fumé and Sancerre.

Reds

Languedoc-Roussillon is the hub of experimentation in France. Here, rich and juicy red wines made from classic grapes such as Syrah/Shiraz, Grenache and Carignan, are easy to drink and can be easy on the wallet, too.

ITALY

Whites

All across the north of the country, from Piedmont to Friuli, Italy is a melting pot of zingy and refreshing whites made from local grapes with personality and attitude. Grapes such as floral Arneis and Friulano or the waxy, appley Ribolla Gialla.

Reds

The days of southern Italy churning out masses of bulk red wine are changing. Instead, carefully crafted, inky-dark, spicy reds are being made from local grapes, such as the dark and brooding Aglianico in Campania, or the meaty grapes Nero di Troia and Negroamaro from Puglia.

SPAIN

Whites

Although Albariño is delicious and perfect with seafood, look out for crisp and fruity white wines made from Verdejo in Rueda, Godello in Valdeorras and the modern take on white Rioja, which is less oaky.

Reds

In north-west Spain, a local grape called Mencía has come of age in the region of Bierzo. It's full of black fruits with a spicy flavour – a great new-wave alternative if you're stuck in a red Rioja rut.

PORTUGAL
Whites
Vinho Verde is more than just retro-cool; it's now making some seriously delicious white wines. The Loureiro grape used here is floral while Alvarinho is richer, and these are the two grapes worth looking out for. The Douro Valley is also a haven for pretty, citrus-fresh white wines made from local grapes.
Reds
Speaking of the Douro Valley, it's also making terrific red wines from the same grape varieties you'd find in the region's most famous wine, Port. I'm talking about Touriga Nacional and Tinta Roriz (Tempranillo). These table reds have a very pure blackberry character with lovely, dry spice flavours of cumin and cinnamon.

AUSTRIA
Blaufränkisch Say it: blauw-fran-kish
This local Austrian red grape varies from very light (in a Beaujolais style) to rich and spicy. I think it's especially tasty when it's lighter and quaffable.

The new New World
As the New World wine countries evolve, they're branching out from the wines and grapes that initially made them famous. This evolution is happening because, as the regions age, the locals have a better understanding of their land's potential with other grapes, plus they're determined to prove to the world they can perfect more than just one style or grape!

AUSTRALIA
Australians are now using 'other' European grapes partly to boost their sophistication credentials. In warmer regions like McLaren Vale, you'll find varieties such as Sicily's Nero d'Avola and Spain's Tempranillo.

NEW ZEALAND
New Zealand is working hard to show it's more than a one-trick (Sauvignon Blanc) or even two-trick (Pinot Noir) pony. With red wine, Syrah/Shiraz is the most exciting grape, especially in Waiheke Island and Hawke's Bay. Meanwhile, many regions are making great Chardonnay and Riesling.

CHILE
Chilean wine is a hive of experimentation. Merlot made it famous but today, Syrah/Shiraz, Carignan and Malbec are worth trying, while the whites are fresh and zesty.

CHINA
Let's wait and see, but China continues its drive to be a wine force to be reckoned with. Grenache is playing its part – apparently lots is being planted. Watch this space.

Blends
Originally, New World wines traded on their easy-to-understand credentials. This included championing wines made from a single grape variety (varietal wines), which was proudly splashed across the wine bottle's front label. This pushed grape varieties into the limelight, but no one, not even the New World guys, ever claimed these varietal wines were superior to blended wines, and yet the world started to think they were. Some of the most prized, expensive and serious wines in the world are actually blends, so don't dismiss them.

A bit of label logic

The labels on New World wine bottles lead with grape variety, and we love this easy way of telling us exactly what's inside the bottle. In fact, it's so popular that Old World countries have started tweaking their labelling laws to (sometimes) allow grape varieties on their labels as well.

France: Know your crus

'Cru' translates as 'growth' in English, and the quality categories of Grand and Premier Cru are used in the French wine regions of Burgundy and Alsace, but also in Champagne, albeit in a different way. Although each region has its own little quirks about what determines the level of cru, Grand Cru is always top dog, followed by Premier Cru. Eating out? On wine lists you'll commonly see Grand Cru shortened to 'GC', and Premier Cru shortened to 'PC' or '1er Cru'.

Bordeaux: Classifications

One part of the Bordeaux region is called the Médoc, and this is where Cabernet Sauvignon reigns supreme. Sometimes, the Médoc is called 'the Left Bank', in relation to the rivers Gironde and Garonne. The Left Bank of Bordeaux has a châteaux hierarchy that was created in 1855, and it still exists today. The '1855 classification', as it is known, ranks Bordeaux châteaux and there are five levels. At the pinnacle are the esteemed and pricey First Growths, with only five châteaux in this top tier. On Bordeaux's Right Bank, Merlot reigns supreme, and this is where you find the village St-Emilion, which also has its own classification system. The most prestigious of these is Premier Grand Cru Classé, which is sub-divided again into two tiers, A and B. Then comes Grand Cru Classé.

Italy: To riserva or non-riserva

'Riserva' usually indicates a producer's higher-quality wine – a wine that has been aged for a longer period than non-riserva wines. It can also mean higher alcohol.

Germany: Name by name

Still plagued by the sweetness tag, if you want to know the style of German Riesling, look out for these labels:
KABINETT *Say it: ka-been-et* dry wine
SPÄTLESE *Say it: shpate-lay-zer* dry or slightly sweet wine
AUSLESE *Say it: owz-lay-zer* sweet-ish wine
BEERENAUSLESE (BA) *Say it: bear-ein-owz-lay-zer* sweet wine
TROCKENBEERENAUSLESE (TBA) *Say it: trok-en-bear-ein-owz-lay-zer* even sweeter wine
EISWEIN *Say it: ice-vine* super-sweet wine

Spain: Rank your reserva

Spanish red wines are often labelled by reserva. Each indicates an ageing period, some of which is in oak:
GRAN RESERVA aged for a minimum of 5 years
RESERVA RED WINES aged for a minimum of 3 years
RESERVA WHITE WINES aged for a minimum of 2 years

Good label innovations

1. QR codes or those little tags you can rip off a bottle's back label. Both of these help us to remember the name of a wine you've drunk while out and about.
2. The Riesling sweetness scale. Riesling is still riddled by an identity crisis because people are wary of it being too sweet. This label is a universal scale printed on the back of bottles.

the
bar

If you just want to crack a bottle open I don't blame you, but this chapter, essentially, covers how to maximize your enjoyment of wine. And it includes just as much everyday stuff, like how to open a bottle of fizz without wasting any when the cork flies across the room or why wine pros hold the glasses by their stems, as it does wine geekery, like the best temperature to serve different styles. Whatever you use it for, The Bar is there to help you get more out of wine.

temperature

Serving wine

Although wine pros can get sniffy about the correct serving temperature of their wine, it's not for affectation, because chilling can have many effects on wine, limiting its smells, reducing the sensation of alcohol sweetness, as well as boosting savoury flavours and tannic texture. As a result, the precise temperature to serve a wine is really down to personal preference and how *you* want *your* wine to taste, but that's not to say a few guidelines aren't helpful!

Remember that old-school serving rules – whites should be served from-the-fridge cold, and all reds should be room-temperature – are misleading and have changed, because the room temperature advice harks back to the days before central heating, when rooms were generally much cooler than they are today. For more on chilling red wines, see page 31.

More complex wines and ones that are slightly older are generally served a little warmer than younger, simpler wines, because the extra warmth allows the oxygen to reach the compounds of the wine, causing them to open and release the flavour.

Another way of looking at it is that if you were serving a very cheap wine (although I'm sure you wouldn't!) or you feel obliged to drink a guest's wine at dinner but don't like the look of it (let's face it, we've all been there), the best solution is to chill it down because it will mute the flavours.

But if you can't decide on the exact temperature to serve a wine, it's always best to serve it on the side of being too cool rather than too warm, because it's much easier and quicker to warm a wine up than to go through the rigmarole of quickly chilling one down.

Despite my saying it's all down to preference, some people like a bit of guidance, so I've provided some, opposite. But don't forget: this isn't the be-all-and-end-all; there's definite room for manoeuvre by a couple of degrees here or there. It's not like anyone's going to get their thermometer out and test that you're getting it right, although there are plenty of temperature gadgets and gizmos out there (see Resources on page 172) if you really do want to keep track of things.

Storing wine

This can be as high- or low-maintenance as you choose. If you have expensive wines and want them to last for the longest time possible, it's best NOT to keep them next to an oven, in the garage, in full sunlight, or under strong UV lighting – never buy a dusty bottle behind a shop counter! Each of these things is either responsible for fluctuating conditions or speeding up the ageing process of the wine. Remember, too, that clear glass lets UV rays through more (therefore speeding up its ageing) than brown or green glass.

THE IDEAL CONDITIONS FOR STORING WINE:
- A cool, dark place
- Constant temperature
- 50–60% humidity, to prevent the corks (if the bottles have corks) from drying out
- Bottles on their side, again, to prevent corks from drying out

Wine cabinets & chillers

Often nicknamed 'fridges', these chillers are the optimum storage solution for those of us who don't have hulking great cellars at home. Specifically designed for wine (as opposed to domestic fridges), they provide all the necessary conditions for storing wine and come in all shapes and sizes so they can fit into whatever space you have available. Liebherr, EuroCave and Caple are three good brands.

Wine style	Temperature
Sparkling	5-8°C (40-45°F)
Aromatic, simple, light white	8°C (45°F)
White	10°C (50°F)
Rich, mature white	12°C (54°F)
Rosé	8-10°C (45-50°F)
Aromatic, simple, light red	12°C (54°F)
Red	14°C (57°F)
Rich, mature red	16°C (60°F)
Light, floral sweet	8°C (45°F)
Rich, honeyed sweet	11°C (52°F)
Fortified	Varies with age and sweetness level

wine props

Opening

THE FOIL

Cutting the foil can be as simple as you want it to be. If you're in a hurry, most corkscrews will just pierce the foil and the cork will pull through it, but that leaves rough and jagged edges. The most common way of trimming the foil is using a foil cutter, which is a little horseshoe-shaped device that is widely available.

To remove the foil, place the cutter over the top of the bottle and twist it back and forth – the foil head should cut off cleanly.

Some foil cutters, however, only cut the foil at the top of the lip that you'll find on most wine bottlenecks. In the wine trade, the common place to cut the foil is at the bottom of this lip, which is often achieved by using the little knife on foldaway corkscrews.

REMOVING CORKS

Corkscrews come in all shapes, sizes and brands these days, so it's down to our choice of style, price and functionality. The two most popular are the lever model and the foldaway Waiter's Friend®.

The lever model is popular and fast, but not a space-saver. The enormous levers of this corkscrew clasp the top of the wine bottle and pull the cork through with hardly any effort at all. Then you reverse the pulling action to remove the cork from the device. It works brilliantly with natural corks, but I've had many sticky moments trying to remove plastic corks from one of these.

A Waiter's Friend® is cheaper, and the most common. As the name suggests, it's a foldaway corkscrew that's widely used in the wine and restaurant trade. It's strong, durable and needs a teeny bit of effort, but not much. Plus, it has a little knife to cut the foil as well as a crown cap bottle opener.

CORK RETRIEVER

This is a little prong-like device aimed at rescuing parts of a cork that have broken off mid-opening. It's not a necessity by any means, but could be useful, especially if you have a collection of older wines. Or you could use a fondue fork instead!

Opening sparkling wine

If a sparkling wine isn't chilled enough or it's been shaken before opening, it will be noisy and messy to open. For a seamless, quiet opening, remove the foil – usually there's a little tab on the foil to help – untwist and loosen the wire cage that covers the cork, then firmly grab the top of the bottle with your writing hand, the base of the bottle with the other, and slowly twist your hands in different directions until you feel the cork loosen. It might not come naturally at first, but practice definitely makes perfect with this.

Before serving

DECANTING

Like with corkscrews, decanters also come in all shapes, sizes and brands, and although you can get something imposing and impressive, a lot of decanting is done for practical rather than aesthetic reasons. There's no right or wrong here, but if you have specific requirements then buy your decanter from a glassware specialist and ask for advice.

Complex wines, whether they're sparkling, white, red, sweet or fortified, benefit from decanting, because the process involves exposing the wine to the air, and contact with oxygen releases a wine's aroma. I say 'complex' wines, because wines that are light in character just won't improve in a decanter – they have nothing more to give.

If you're decanting to catch sediment – which will rule out most white and sparkling wines – the best

fragile – I'm talking about, say, a 50-year-old red Burgundy), then it needs to be decanted and served almost immediately rather than left to sit in a decanter for an hour or more. This kind of wine would be so delicate its aroma and flavour could get totally lost if sitting around in a decanter for too long, so take care.

Cleaning decanters
The nooks and crannies inside a decanter can be a nightmare to clean and dry, but there are a few neat little inventions that can help. These include specialist glass brushes, cleaning fluids and metal cleaning balls.

I'm a big fan of drying crystals: silica crystals are held within what looks like a fabric snake that absorbs any moisture inside the decanter.

It's also useful to swill your decanter with a little water or wine each time before you fill it up again, discarding the water or wine, to remove any impurities.

After it's been opened

There are loads of ways we can attempt to keep a wine going (to stop it from oxidizing). The most basic way is to re-cork and chill it in the fridge. It's not useless but it's cheap and the least effective. A more technical option is to spray argon gas (available in a tube like a hairspray cannister) into the bottle. This inert and odourless gas is heavier than air and when sprayed across the surface of the wine, it prevents oxidization.

The new kid on the block is the Coravin™ system – a device that's still work in progress but fantastic for sampling older, rarer wines without wasting them. A needle is inserted into the cork to extract the wine, and as the needle enters, the bottle is pressurized with argon gas that forces the wine up through the needle and into a glass.

method is to lay a piece of muslin/cheesecloth over the top of the decanter and pour the wine through the material. If you find muslin/cheesecloth hard to come by, there are alternatives you can use. I often use a tea-leaf strainer, while low-denier tights/stockings can also work as a decanting mesh.

There are no strict rules as to how long you decant the wine before it's served, and it can depend on the temperature you want the wine to be served at. However, if a wine is very old (to the point of being

glassware

If the wine you drink says something about you, then so too does your choice of wine glass. They come in all shapes, sizes, costs and colours, and while most serious wine glasses are clear, some also now come in black to remove the potential for any prejudice by a professional taster (many of whom will refer to glasses as 'stemware', or 'stems').

If you mean business with wine, even if you're still a beginner, I'd spend as much as you can on a wine glass, because the quality of the tasting experience – in other words your perception of the wine – really improves with a good-quality glass. I'm pretty relaxed about my choice of glass in general, but, I have to confess I have one go-to favourite and one absolute nemesis.

My go-to favourite ★

A couple of years ago I discovered a weightless glass that could be washed in the dishwasher. In fact, the manufacturer recommends that it should be washed in the dishwasher. Sound too good to be true? Well, it works. This is the Universal glass made by a manufacturer called Zalto, and it's perfect for my daily professional use. Made from titanium crystal (see below) for extra strength, I was astonished when I was first shown this glass as someone just dropped it on the floor and it didn't smash. Incredible.

Lead crystal versus titanium crystal
Recently, manufacturers have started making wine glasses using titanium crystal instead of lead crystal. By replacing the lead oxide with titanium oxide, glasses can't stain or be easily scratched, and are very, very strong.

One to avoid

I could de-snob myself about this if I really wanted to, but there is one glass that I really can't stand, and as much as I love most things with retro-cool cachet, I draw the line at the infamous Paris Goblet. Once a staple wine glass for bistros and public houses, they've slowly been phased out, and I'm not surprised. They look ugly, are impractical (just try swirling a decent glass of wine around without some sloshing over the side) and they don't hold much wine.

Shape & size

If you're interested in fashion over function, this bit isn't for you. But, if you're looking for a wine glass that gets the most out of the wine within it, then it could be worth looking at manufacturers which have different glass shapes for different grape varieties and styles. The pioneer of this revolutionary idea was Claus Riedel, who started making wine glasses this way more than 50 years ago, and the Riedel range is still going strong today (see Resources on page 172). If you only have the budget and space for a few glasses, try to get different ones for sparkling, white, red and fortified wines at least.

RED Usually served with larger bowls because they allow the aromas and flavours of the wine to open out, much in the same way decanting does (see pages 16–17).
WHITE Served in narrower glasses than for red wine, to capture white wine's fresh, fruity flavours.
SPARKLING Traditionally tall and thin, this shape makes the most of the energetic bubbles shooting to the top, but the flute has now started to widen.
FORTIFIED A smaller glass is best, just to emphasize the fruit flavours rather than the higher alcohol. A small version of a white wine glass could do the job.

Trends in glassware

It might sound a bit crazy but, just as there are trends with wine, there are trends with wine glasses.

CHAMPAGNE & FIZZ

Champagne and other high-calibre fizz are increasingly served in wider glasses rather than the classic tall flutes. Even though the narrow flute channels bubbles to the top of the glass, it doesn't make the most of the complexity of these wines. They deserve to open out a bit so you can really enjoy their flavour, which means they need a wider bowl. Many bars and restaurants now use a compromised version; the glass is noticeably taller and thinner than your average wine glass, but it has a wider bowl than it used to, to show off the wine's complexity.

TUMBLERS

'What?' I hear you say. Well, down-to-earth tapas bars and modern restaurants often now serve still wine in little glass tumblers. I quite like this rebellious take on serving wine, especially as it removes the snobbery from drinking wine. The only downside is that you can't swirl the wine around for a good sniff.

Holding a wine glass correctly

I always get asked about this at wine tastings. It's usually best to hold a wine by the stem of the glass to give you better control if you want to swirl and sniff it. But most importantly for a chilled wine, it prevents the heat from your hands warming the wine up too quickly. Red wine glasses can also be held by the stem for the same reasons, but it doesn't matter so much if these warm up a little, so it's not as frowned upon by the wine community.

Before you fill your glass...
Whether you wash your glasses by hand or in the dishwasher, it's always good to rinse them with water or wine before you fill them up. This will get rid of any cleaning product residue, which can seriously affect a wine's performance, dumbing down flavour and aroma, and making sparkling wines go flat.

Same wine, different glass

I've been sceptical about these experiments you often read about. Ones that are done with the same wine and different glasses, even though the conclusion is usually the same – that the shape and material of the 'glass' DOES affect how a wine tastes. So, I conducted a little experiment in my kitchen and it really hit home just how differently a wine can behave and taste when drunk from different vessels. Here are the results.

The experiment

I used a Premier Cru Brut NV Champagne, made from 50% Chardonnay and equal parts Pinot Noir and Pinot Meunier, and seven different containers to drink it from. I especially wanted to use a sparkling wine because I also wanted to see whether the 'glasses' changed the effect of the bubbles. And, just to be fair, I rinsed each glass out with some of the Champagne before using it. I've listed them in order of success, just to give you an idea of how each one performed.

1 CHAMPAGNE FLUTE

No surprises here. This flute was a modern one, so it had a relatively wide bowl, rather than being a tall and thin column-shaped flute, and the Champagne tasted best from it. The wine had a strong aroma – it smelt of lemon cheesecake (citrus and biscuit/cookie) – and the bubbles in the mouth were energetic and precise.

2 SHERRY COPITA

The most similar in shape to the flute, and although the wine wasn't as aromatic, the aromas were still very obvious, albeit with a heavier and richer biscuit/cookie character. Again, in the mouth, the flavour was rich and intense, with that toasty, biscuit/cookie flavour really showing through, plus the bubbles stayed neat and precise rather than foaming up.

3 CERAMIC MUG

Surprised this is third place? I was! This showed a good, toasty Champagne aroma, the fizz was energetic but not foamy, and the flavour was rich.

4 LARGE RED WINE GLASS

The Champagne showed barely any aroma but if you sniffed very hard, it smelt a little bit toasty. The rim had the same effect on the fizz as the glass tumbler (below), it was mega-foamy, so much so it was hard to control in the mouth!

5 GLASS TUMBLER

I could barely smell anything with this. The wide rim of the tumbler really made the bubbles froth up in the mouth, although I could taste some lemon flavours.

6 CHILD'S PLASTIC BEAKER

Completely dead on the nose. Nothing at all. The bubbles were energetic without being foamy but the flavour of the wine was metallic and unpleasant. Definitely not recommended.

7 DISPOSABLE WHITE PLASTIC BEAKER

I gave a deserved no score for this. The wine had no aroma, the bubbles disappeared instantly and there was no flavour.

the
cellar

Get ready. This is where we dive, head first, into all those fantastic grape varieties and discover what they taste like. We're honing in on flavour rather than geography here, so you won't find any maps but you will find photos of all the lovely flavours that each grape conjures up when it's turned into wine. This should give your brain and palate a head start in terms of understanding what that grape's all about. We start with reds and move on to whites, but there's no special ordering of the grapes. And by the way, rosé, sparkling, sweet and fortified wines are listed by style rather than grape as they're much simpler to explain and understand this way.

PICK THE RIGHT WINE: RED & ROSÉ

Whether you know the grape you want, the flavour you are in the mood for, or the food you're eating, we all need a little shortcut at some point in our lives, so this is a quick reference guide for when it's that kind of moment.

red

light

Dolcetto & Barbera → cherry · spice

Cabernet Franc → rhubarb · herbaceous

Pinot Noir & Gamay → raspberry · strawberry

} charcuterie
fish
lamb
pasta
pizza

medium

Syrah/Shiraz → black pepper · blackberry

Merlot → plum · beetroot/beet

Sangiovese → cherry · raspberry · mushroom

Carmenère → chocolate · spice

Blaufränkisch → cherry · beetroot/beet

} beef
cured pork
game
lamb
spicy food

Grenache → plum · blackcurrant

Montepulciano → cherry · black tea

bold

Cabernet Sauvignon → blackcurrant · mint

Tempranillo → meaty · leather

Nebbiolo → black pepper · cherry · mushroom

Malbec → blackcurrant · smoky

Zinfandel → chocolate · liquorice

} beef
game
mushroom

Pinotage → smoky · coffee

Touriga Nacional → blackcurrant · fruit cake

Tannat → oaky · spice

rosé

light

Pinot Noir → strawberry · raspberry

Cabernet Franc → cherry · herbaceous

Merlot → cranberry · strawberry

Grenache → strawberry · pomegranate

} cheese
   fish
   salads
   vegetables

medium-bodied

Syrah/Shiraz → cherry · spice

Cabernet Sauvignon → raspberry · black pepper

Grenache, non-French → strawberry · cream

Touriga Nacional → pomegranate · grapefruit

Negroamaro → cherry · spice

Malbec → pomegranate · strawberry

} barbecues
   fish
   picnics
   spicy food

off-dry

White Zinfandel → strawberry · cream

White Merlot → strawberry · cream

} aperitif
   dessert

pinot noir

perfumed
fresh
juicy
hedonistic
succulent
smooth
earthy
elegant

The diva of wine grapes, Pinot Noir is fussy about where it's grown, and that can push up its price. But when it works well, it's the ultimate in wine hedonism. Pinot Noir usually grows best in cooler climates and produces a pale liquid by red wine standards. It's lovely when young and full of juicy strawberry and red-cherry flavours, but it's also delicious when older, tasting smooth and earthy.

Pinot Noir's home is Burgundy, and winemakers everywhere are completely mesmerized and inspired by the beautiful wine that Pinot Noir makes in this region. Producers everywhere, though, have to be careful not to slather the grape in too much oak or let the alcohol level creep too high because both can spoil this grape's trademark delicacy. Sometimes people refer to Pinot Noir simply as 'Pinot'. You can do this, but tread carefully, as there are plenty of other grapes in the Pinot family, like Pinot Gris and Pinot Blanc.

Pinot Noir is also a vital ingredient in some of the world's best sparkling wines. The pulp of the grape (where the juice comes from) is quickly removed from the skins after harvest so the wine doesn't take on any pink colour from the skins unless you want a rosé. A fizz made entirely from Pinot Noir will often be given the name Blanc de Noirs, roughly translated as white wine made from black grapes. It also makes great pink fizz, and is done one of two ways. The first is to add some red Pinot Noir wine to white Champagne, the other is to let the skin of the grape stay in contact with the wine for enough time to let the colour seep into the wine. This is called *saignée* (bleeding).

🏠 Burgundy, France

Red Burgundy is made from Pinot Noir. That's the easy bit. Napoleonic laws of heritance, based on inheritance by bloodline, have meant that growers' vineyards have been hugely fragmented over the years through generations. For example, one region that's just 50 hectares in size may be shared by 90 growers, all producing wines that are rare, and this contributes to their higher-than-average price. The most revered strip of vineyards in Burgundy is split in two. The southern half, Côte de Beaune, is more Chardonnay territory, but you can still find elegant Pinot Noirs there. The northern half, Côte de Nuits, is Pinot Noir country. The wines here are usually a bit richer than in the south, with a savoury, earthy character as well as plump fruit.

In descending order of prestige, red Burgundy (Pinot Noir) is labelled:
🏆 Grand Cru
• Premier Cru
• (The name of a village), for example Pommard
• (The name of a group of villages), for example Côte de Nuits-Villages
• Bourgogne

This grape...

SMELLS:

herbaceous · perfumed · smoky · toasty

TASTES OF:

beetroot/beet · cherry · cranberry · mushroom · plum · pomegranate · raspberry · rhubarb · strawberry · truffle

" Pinot Noir is one of the most versatile, food-friendly grapes or styles around. It can handle the pungency and strength of garlic and fragrant spices as well as the acidity of tomatoes, the richness of lamb and the delicacy of fish. "

pinot noir: regions & flavours

Italy

Pinot Nero, as it is called locally, thrives in the cool Italian north, near the Alps. Especially so in Alto Adige, where it makes fresh wines with bright cherry flavours. It's also made in Lombardy, where it is essential to the production of the sparkling wine Franciacorta (see pages 126–129).

Germany 👁

Spätburgunder, as it's known locally, is becoming increasingly important in Germany. There's a lot more of it around now than there was even 15 years ago, although admittedly it's still not the easiest thing to track down. It's more popular in the South, in regions like Baden and Pfalz, where it's warm enough to ripen properly. These wines are delicate, and come from vines on schist-based soils that give a stony, slate-like flavour to them. In other words, they're usually savoury styles of Pinot Noir, rather than those that are full of juicy fruit. They're hugely underestimated, very classy, and I'm tipping them to be something to watch for in years to come. A word of warning though – they can be pricey.

USA

There are a few great little pockets of Pinot Noir expertise in the United States. In California, Russian River Valley and Los Carneros do a delicious job. Californian Pinot Noir is usually bigger and fruitier in style than many other Pinot Noir-producing regions, and Los Carneros makes excellent sparkling wines as well as red Pinot Noir. In Oregon, Pinot Noir is the flagship grape, and the Oregon sub-region of Willamette Valley excels in making it. Here, the wines are elegant and perfumed, and those I really enjoy come from Domaine Drouhin, Bergstrom and Cristom.

Chile

Chile produces real value-for-money, young and juicy Pinot Noir, especially from the now-renowned regions of Casablanca and San Antonio. The sophistication of its Pinot Noirs is growing all the time, especially when made from cooler, newish spots like Leyda and Paradones. Cono Sur makes many levels of Pinot Noir and the range is always consistently good. Viña Mar was one of the Chilean Pinot Noir pioneers and still makes great Pinots today. Casa Real also makes fantastic wine in Paradones, while Viña Leyda makes fresh, coastal Pinot Noir that is fruity but with a distinct salty kick.

New Zealand

The cool, maritime New Zealand climate is great for Pinot Noir and, a bit like Chardonnay, it is made consistently well in lots of regions. Historically, Martinborough was the region with the best reputation, and it still makes excellent Pinot Noirs from producers like Ata Rangi and Craggy Range.

However, the region that makes the biggest splash with top-end NZ Pinot Noir these days is Central Otago. This is the most southerly wine-producing region in the world. It makes achingly beautiful Pinot Noir, and is destined for even greater things in years to

chill down

If you're serving Pinot Noir with fish, or as a lighter summer wine, don't be afraid to chill it for 15 minutes in the fridge. The bright fruit will taste extra-fresh with a touch of chill to it. See page 31 for more information.

come. The wines are dense in cherry fruit flavours, with a gentle, toasty richness and delicate spice; it's really serious stuff. There's an iconic producer here, too, in Felton Road, and while these wines are delicious, other producers I like very much include Mount Edward, Rippon, Doctors Flat and Burn Cottage.

Marlborough also makes delicious Pinot Noir with raspberry and cherry fruit, and a delicate savoury character as well. Some of the most serious (and gorgeous!) I know are from Dog Point and Seresin.

Eastern Europe

Sounds crazy? Perhaps. But there's no denying that Bulgaria, Romania and Hungary are places to watch for good-value Pinot Noir. And, although they're on-the-up in terms of easy-drinking and light Pinot Noirs, these countries haven't shown any signs of competing with complex Pinot Noir-producing regions. Yet. The best I have tasted so far comes from Bulgaria and a producer called Edoardo Miroglio.

The rest of France

Let's not forget the Loire Valley for Pinot Noir. Red Sancerre, especially, makes gorgeous Pinot Noirs to drink in spring and summer. They're vibrant, perky and fresh. I especially like those from Vincent Delaporte and Gérard et Pierre Morin.

Alsace, which has a pretty cool climate, makes a similarly savoury style of Pinot Noir to those from Baden in Germany, which is just across the border. And even though it's much warmer, we're now seeing ripe and juicy Pinot Noir coming from the south of France, although it's not a natural home for it, and at the moment, that warmth shows in the wines.

Chilling red wine

Here's the thing; chilling red wine isn't done anywhere near enough. Over the years we've been conditioned into thinking red wines need to be served at room temperature, but this is a modern-day fallacy because this advice was dished out in the time pre-central heating, when rooms were generally a lot cooler. Which means that very few red wines taste their best at today's version of room temperature. Plus, some grape varieties show even better when the wines taste fresher and spicier, and this is easily achieved by chilling a red wine. Not everyone wants their wine to taste that way, I get that, but it can be a really lovely way to drink red wine, especially in the summer. The best 'chill-able' red wines have low tannin and alcohol.

Reds you can serve straight from the fridge

BEAUJOLAIS & BEAUJOLAIS NOUVEAU (MADE WITH GAMAY) These are the two most basic levels of Beaujolais. Beaujolais Nouveau is sold in November each year as a very young wine and is super-fruity.

LAMBRUSCO A slightly sparkling Italian wine that's brilliant with pizza.

Reds you can serve 15 minutes after leaving the fridge

BEAUJOLAIS-VILLAGES & BEAUJOLAIS CRU (MADE WITH GAMAY) Cru is the highest quality category of Beaujolais, which is less fruity than cheaper Beaujolais, but still fruity enough to be chilled happily.

PINOT NOIR Choose lighter styles of Pinot Noir from cooler places, when they're fruity and unoaked.

CABERNET FRANC Famous for its green herbal aroma, this grape often tastes best when served cool. Those from the Loire Valley are especially good.

ZWEIGELT *Say it: Sv-eye-gelt* Austria's lightest and perkiest red grape loves having a chilly edge to it.

FRAPPATO A very juicy, light and jammy-fresh wine made mostly in the south of Italy.

SWEET REDS It's good to serve sweet red wines chilled, because it balances out the wine's sweetness.

BOBAL An up-and-coming Spanish grape that's supple and very fruity.

MENCÍA Another up-and-coming Spanish grape with a floral perfume that's accentuated when served cool.

SPARKLING SHIRAZ You'd normally serve fizz cold, wouldn't you? So treat the bubbles in this wine the same way. The ripe Shiraz fruit will need some time to open out, so it's best to leave it a few minutes to warm up, rather than serve it straight from the fridge.

Reds to serve 30 minutes or more after leaving the fridge

GRENACHE This grape is low in tannin so it's often happy being a bit cooler. The younger the better, and for me this usually applies more to New World Grenache wines than those from Spain or France.

SYRAH/SHIRAZ Although Syrah can be high in tannin, the floral aroma and black-pepper spice is beautifully accentuated if it's served cool. Syrah from the Elqui Valley in Chile is a classic example.

MANSOIS Reds from the pocket of Marcillac in south-west France make lovely, crunchy red wines from Mansois that cry out to be a little cold because of their subtle spice.

what is 'cellar cold'?

It's just a phrase used in the wine trade to describe a wine that is noticeably cooler to the touch than room temperature, without being fridge-cold.

syrah/shiraz

rich

spicy

smoky

peppery

meaty

perfumed

elegant

Want to know how a Syrah or Shiraz is going to taste? Just look at its name. Syrah used to be the name exclusively used for this grape in the Old World, while the New World favoured Shiraz. Now, winemakers in the New World often think their wines have the panache and style (some might say 'elegance') of the Old World Syrahs, so now they're also starting to call their wines Syrah instead of Shiraz. This means that the name on the label gives an indication of the style of Syrah/Shiraz it's going to be. Shiraz in its classic form is big and ballsy, jammed with black fruits, but then also crammed with a hit of black pepper, spice and liquorice. Syrah, on the other hand, is a much more genteel affair. It still has plenty of black fruit, but it's often tamed with a mushroom-flavoured earthy character.

Syrah/Shiraz is just as tasty when its made on its own as it is when it's blended with other grapes in a wine. Some of its favourite blending partners are Grenache and Mourvèdre, but you can also find it blended with Cabernet Sauvignon. And then one of its classic blending partners is actually Viognier, a white grape. Classy, flavoursome, versatile; that's Syrah/Shiraz.

🏠 Rhône Valley, France

The east strip of France that runs southwards from Lyon to Avignon is a Mecca for Syrah. In wine terms, the Rhône is split in two: north and south. In the north, Lyon to Montélimar, Syrah is the only red grape allowed, although it's often blended with the white Viognier grape here. In the south, Syrah is blended with a fanfare of other grapes, such as Grenache, Mourvèdre and Cinsault. Famous wine regions and styles here, such as Gigondas and Châteauneuf-du-Pape, are usually made from Syrah blends. These wines are big and bold, and can be quite tannic when young, but the good ones can age for many years. A classic aroma and taste description for these particular Syrahs is smoky bacon.

The Lowdown on Syrah/Shiraz

A red grape with a pedigree, originally from the Rhône Valley in France, it's just as easy to find this blended with other grapes as a single-grape variety. It can be drunk when young, but high-quality styles also age well.

This grape...
SMELLS:
**herbaceous · oaky ·
smoky · toasty**
TASTES OF:
**aniseed · bacon · black
olive · black pepper ·
blackcurrant · cherry ·
chocolate · coffee ·
currants · eucalyptus ·
fruit cake · jam/jelly ·
nuts · plum ·
raspberry · rosemary ·
thyme**

syrah/shiraz: regions & flavours

Australia

Most Australians opt for the name Shiraz, and although the quality can range from basic to mind-blowingly good, I think it's been victim of its own success. While the blockbuster-spicy, fruit-bomb Shiraz took the world by storm in the late 1990s, most people now (wrongly) assume that all Australian Shiraz is too big to handle. This definitely isn't the case. So give it another go, please! The region that's really held up on a pedestal for its Shiraz is Barossa Valley, in South Australia. These wines can command an eye-watering price but they're often worth it. Because it is the signature red grape, Shiraz is popular all over Australia, although the overworked, soupy, over-alcoholic versions that made it notorious are far less common now. Essentially, Australian Shiraz comes down to this: lovely, ripe blackcurrant fruit, a lick of spice and liquorice with a hit of eucalyptus. Look to Barossa for polished panache, McLaren Vale for punchy power, and Victoria for genteel elegance. Some of my favourite Australian Shiraz producers are Clonakilla, Teusner and Jasper Hill.

South Africa 👁

South Africa is beginning to look like hot property for Syrah/Shiraz and its constant improvement in quality is really helping to raise the reputation of this country's red wine scene, one that has previously been slighted by red wines with a burnt-rubber aroma and flavour. That problem seems to be much less widespread these days. Of all the countries that name the wines Syrah/Shiraz, perhaps South Africa is the most split when it comes to choosing what to call it. The most exciting South African region for Syrah at the moment is Swartland, just north of Cape Town, where all (okay, most of) the hip, cool, up-and-coming winemakers are making some seriously sophisticated wines. Mullineux makes some gorgeous, and very serious Syrah/Shiraz here. For classic South African Shiraz, try wines from Stellenbosch. The good ones have a purity and lusciousness to the fruit, with lots of dark/bittersweet chocolate flavours: big, ripe and juicy.

Chile

Watch out for Chilean Syrah/Shiraz – it's important for Chile's high-quality wine scene. Of course there's still work to do, but the newly discovered regions in northern Chile are really helping Syrah/Shiraz's cause, especially in the Elqui Valley, where Syrah/Shiraz is the signature grape. I've found these wines to be pure in black fruit with a cool, black-pepper edge. Pretty classy stuff for a region that's still so new. Only a handful of producers exist, but my tip for now is to try the wines of Viña Falernia.

New Zealand

This is Syrah/Shiraz with a cool-climate twist, and is, like in Chile, still not produced in huge quantities, but when it's made here, it's usually very good. I like the reserved style, with the crushed black-pepper spice that the cooler temperature brings to the flesh of the wine. Hawkes Bay and Waiheke Island are making awesome Syrah/Shiraz styles. Try Trinity Hill and The Hay Paddock.

viognier blends
Syrah/Shiraz and the white grape Viognier are very happy bedfellows – so much so, this is quite a classic wine style. See pages 72–75 for more on blending Syrah/Shiraz with Viognier.

cabernet sauvignon

plush
concentrated
smoky
meaty
chewy

Packed with flavour, high quality and relatively easy to grow, Cabernet Sauvignon is one of the world's most important grapes. It is one of the true and original 'international' wine grapes, too, because it's grown and made into wine very successfully all over the world.

Cabernet Sauvignon is French, of course, but it is not native to the region of Bordeaux as so many people think. True, Bordeaux is the region that made Cabernet Sauvignon famous, but it actually comes from further down the country, in south-west France. Plus, and this is unusual for some of the best-known grapes, both of its parent grapes are big players in the world of wine in their own right: Cabernet Franc and Sauvignon Blanc.

It might feel like the safe option, buying a bottle of Cabernet Sauvignon, but it has way more going for it than just brand recognition. The dark skin of the berries gives the wine a strong colour; their thick skin adds tannin and grip in the mouth (which can help a wine to age) and it loves to be blended. Some red grapes and styles can be flabby and soft in the mouth when they are grown and made in warm climates, but not Cab Sauv, which has a naturally high acidity that keeps its wines fresh in the mouth. It's also a huge bonus that Cabernet Sauvignon can be just as good by itself as it is when it's part of a blend.

Merlot is one of Cabernet Sauvignon's all-time-favourite blending partners, and together they're a fantastic match. Bordeaux is where this blend is most famously made, but it's found everywhere, from West Coast USA to Italy.

Although Cabernet Sauvignon has many high-quality credentials, that's not to say all of its wines are the pinnacle of red wine production. Cabernet Sauvignon is often made into flavoursome cheaper (more affordable) wines, too, which goes some way to explaining its popularity.

🏠 South-west France

There's isn't one location you can point to and say, 'Look; this is where Cabernet Sauvignon rules.' Instead, Cabernet Sauvignon makes itself useful across many of the sub-regions in south-west France, including those around the fringes of Bordeaux, like Bergerac, and further south in places like Madiran. In wines from these regions, a dollop of Cabernet Sauvignon in the blend can add colour, pedigree, potential longevity. You name it, Cabernet Sauvignon can improve it. Usually...

This grape...

SMELLS:
smoky · toasty · oaky
· leathery

TASTES OF:
blackcurrant ·
blueberry · cherry ·
cinnamon · eucalyptus
· fruit cake · jam/jelly
· liquorice · mint ·
nutmeg · prune ·
tobacco · vanilla

cabernet sauvignon:
regions & flavours

Bordeaux, France
This isn't just for collectors and millionaires; Cabernet Sauvignon is one of the linchpins of red Bordeaux at all quality and price levels. And remember, all red Bordeaux is given the name 'claret', no matter what it is or how much it costs. It hardly ever flies solo here, though, and is usually blended with Bordeaux's 'other' red grapes, such as Merlot and Cabernet Franc.

Oak and Cabernet Sauvignon are good friends, because the grape's fruit is ballsy enough to take on a fair whack of oak, but be careful with young wines as they can sometimes be quite strong in oaky tannin and therefore taste charred. Cabernet Sauvignon vineyards thrive in the part of Bordeaux known as the Left Bank (of the River Gironde). On the Right Bank, the soils are more suitable for Merlot, although both grapes exist on both banks. When Cabernet Sauvignon dominates in a claret, it's famously powerful with blackcurrant and mint aromas and flavours.

USA
The backbone of California's serious wine reputation was built on Cabernet Sauvignon. It was made famous in the 1970s, when a blind-tasting competition of California versus Bordeaux ('The Judgement of Paris') revealed the Californian wines fared better in the results. It caused serious shockwaves through the wine community, much to the delight of the Americans and, unsurprisingly, since then, the Cabernet Sauvignon wine scene in California has gone crazy, exploded, especially in the highfalutin regions of Napa and Sonoma. These wines are usually hefty beasts that pack quite a punch, with big tannins that need time to soften out. These are food wines, make no mistake. In Washington State, the USA's other main Cabernet

Sauvignon hub, I usually find it less in-your-face and more fruity. The top wines are ready for drinking earlier, usually because they have less tannin. This state is definitely the place to eke out some undiscovered Cabernet Sauvignon-producing gems like Hedge's, Woodward Canyon, K Vintners and Leonetti Cellars.

Australia
Cabernet Sauvignon is one of the major red wines that helped Australia make a name for itself, and in fairness, decent, easy-drinking Cabernet Sauvignon can be found everywhere. Big in rich fruit with blackcurrant cordial-like concentration, a lot of Australian Cabernet Sauvignon (or 'Aussie Cab', as it's known) is blended with Merlot or Shiraz. Even when it's blended here, though, it retains a really distinctive character of blueberry and blackcurrant fruit, but the most obvious flavours are mint and eucalyptus.

A fashionable place to seek out top-end Cabernet Sauvignon at the moment is in Western Australia, especially the region of Margaret River, which makes very elegant wines, such as those from Cullen Wines. Less fashionable, but still hugely respected as an area for serious Cabernet Sauvignon, is Coonawarra in South Australia. Katnook is a particular favourite producer of mine.

China 👁
Surprised to see this here? Well, because red Bordeaux has won over so many Chinese wine drinkers in recent years, they're having a crack at it themselves, and so the rate of vine planting has rocketed. If you have a chance to try these wines I'd really recommend it. That said, China hasn't proven itself to have ideal

 Cabernet Sauvignon is often shortened to Cabernet, or just 'Cab Sauv', even though there are other important grapes out there beginning with Cabernet, like Cabernet Franc.

growing conditions for Cabernet Sauvignon just yet. But the appetite for success is huge, and experienced winemakers are being drafted in from all over the world to help improve China's wine quality. It's a question of watch this space – at the moment, the region of Ningxia looks like it has the most potential.

Chile

Cabernet Sauvignon grows especially well in Chile, so many producers here have a Cabernet Sauvignon wine in their range. Today, as Chile continues to experiment successfully with other grapes, and discover on a more specific basis what regions are suited to particular

grapes, easy-going Cabernet Sauvignon is less of a focus for them, although there's no denying that Cabernet Sauvignon makes very fruity, flavoursome and usually affordable wines here. Casa Lapostolle, Viña von Siebenthal, Errázuriz, De Martino and Valdivieso wines would be on my shopping list.

The rest of Europe

France aside, Cabernet Sauvignon is a major player for some big names in Italy, especially central and southern Italy (although local grape varieties still rule here, naturally). Most famously, Cabernet Sauvignon is big in Tuscany, where it's crucial for the wines known modestly as the 'Super Tuscans'. Back in the 1960s, Super Tuscan producers decided to make wines from international grapes like Cabernet Sauvignon and Merlot, which meant they couldn't qualify for Italy's traditional quality hierarchy system. This rebellion made Cabernet Sauvignon infamous and guaranteed its place on the Italian wine scene. Plus, the wines are excellent, so they're now a firm fixture in Tuscany – and the Tuscans can charge quite a price for them, too. The most famous Super Tuscan, and for including a lot of Cabernet Sauvignon, is Sassicaia, but I'm also a huge fan of the lesser-known Castello del Terriccio Super Tuscan, called Lupicaia.

Cabernet Sauvignon is also grown throughout Spain, and is sometimes used in red Rioja, although not in large quantities. Spanish Cabernet Sauvignon is big and meaty, I usually find it to be somewhere between Bordeaux and California in style and weight in the mouth.

Let's talk tannin...

Tannin is that dry, chewy coating you feel in the mouth when you take a sip of wine. It clings to teeth, the tongue and the sides of the mouth and has the same effect as tea that's had the teabag in it for too long.

Where does tannin come from?

GRAPES It's naturally present in the stems, skins and seeds of a grape. The level of tannin is usually higher in black/red grapes than white grapes.

WOOD Wines that spend time in contact with wood will pick up more tannin. When the wood is brand new, the tannin presence in wine is stronger. However, when winemakers use 'old' barrels – ones that previously contained wine – the tannin strength is weaker.

What does it do?

Tannin acts as a frame for a wine to develop around. It provides a chewy texture in the mouth and can improve a wine's ability to age. That's not to say that all wines that have massive tannins are going to age well for decades, just that tannin is one of the crucial components for ageing.

Want to feel less tannin?

There are two really easy ways to minimize tannin. One is to drink the wine with food. The texture of food in your mouth will lessen the chewy impact of tannin. The other is to age the wine. Tannins dissipate with time, but you have to bear in mind whether the wine has the rest of the attributes to age well – big tannins alone don't constitute a high-quality wine.

Why put wine in wood in the first place?

For two simple reasons: flavour and tannin. The flavour of wood can be critical to a wine's trademark style, as it is in red Rioja or Napa Cabernet Sauvignon. Wine can be aged in wood or fermented in wood. For maximum flavour of the wood and tannin strength, a winemaker will do both. Oak is far and away the most popular wood used in winemaking because the flavour it imparts to the wine is favourable, but also because it's more watertight than other varieties of wood.

Where does the oak come from?

France and America are by far the most popular locations for sourcing oak for wine. Winemakers choose the origin of their oak based on how it will affect the wine's taste. For example, historically, red Rioja producers have always preferred American oak, but in Italy, Slavonian oak from Bosnia, Slovenia and Serbia is popular for grape varieties like Nebbiolo. American oak has a hallmark flavour of vanilla that isn't as prominent in French oak.

Do you have to use barrels?

No. A cheaper way to introduce oak influence is to suspend oak chips or oak staves (planks) in the wine, like a teabag. However, this method is widely deemed an inferior method, compared with using oak barrels.

How do barrels change the flavour?

The barrels are exposed to fire and 'toasted'. Generally, there are three levels of toasting – light, medium and strong. The stronger the toast level, the more the flavour of the barrel will show through in the wine.

Did you know?

Tannins in wine taste stronger to us when we drink wine on a flight because altitude accentuates our perception of tannin.

merlot

juicy
succulent
smooth
creamy
spicy

Merlot has plenty going for it; it's easy to pronounce, easy to drink and can be easy on the wallet, too. Merlot actually has two identities, though. It has enough character to make fleshy, fruity, easy-drinking red wines on its own (known as a single-varietal wine). It has this character because Merlot berries are relatively large, which means the juice-to-skin ratio is high, giving its wines extra-fleshy red-fruit flavour, like those you find in Chile. Or, Merlot can be an important component in blended wines, which include some of the most expensive wines in the world, like red Bordeaux, which is also known as claret, or the Super Tuscans (see page 40).

The 'wing man' role that Merlot plays to Cabernet Sauvignon is seriously important, because Cabernet Sauvignon can sometimes taste a bit tight on its own and needs fleshing out, making Merlot the perfect partner. Whether used as part of a blend (with any grape by the way, not just Cab Sauv), or on its own, Merlot is grown all over the world, because it's popular to drink and relatively easy to grow, making it, like Cabernet Sauvignon, another of these 'international' grapes.

🏠 Bordeaux, France

On Bordeaux's Right Bank, where the soils are rich in clay, Merlot takes charge. It doesn't just make expensive wines from châteaux like Petrus, Angélus and Cheval Blanc; but it can and does make everyday wines, rich in black plum flavours. Merlot also plays a vital support act to Cabernet Sauvignon in making some of the most admired and expensive wines in the world. These include the First Growths in the part of Bordeaux known as the Left Bank (see page 11). Here, Merlot softens Cabernet Sauvignon to boost the fruit flavour in the wines.

Did you know?
Merlot was dealt a blow after the film 'Sideways' came out a few years ago, because it was passed off as an inferior grape to Pinot Noir. BUT Merlot is one of the two most important grapes in Château Cheval Blanc, the wine that was landed as the pinnacle of wine refinement at the end of the film!

This grape...
SMELLS:
gamey · leathery · smoky
TASTES OF:
beetroot/beet · black olive · cedar · cigar · eucalyptus · fruit cake · liquorice · plum · vanilla

merlot: regions & flavours

Chile

Chilean Merlot is a signature style that put Chile on the winemaking map. With tons of fruit, a soft texture and light tannins, it's uncomplicated and often very affordable. Merlot contributed to Chile's reputation as a country that could only produce cheap quaffing wines but that's changed a lot in recent years, as Chile has branched out, growing a wide variety of grapes, including many of those featured in this book. Chilean Merlot is still big business, though, and a lot of the wines are in the affordable style, packed with lots of fruit, and that still makes them a winner in many people's books. See below for its famous confusion with Carmenère.

Italy

Although other countries are scaling back on Merlot, it's become increasingly important in Italy in recent years. You'll find most Italian Merlot in the north of the country. It's not massively identifiable in Italy because it is usually blended with other grapes. Plus, of course, it is most important for its role as part of the famous (and infamous!) production of Super Tuscan wines (see page 40).

Spain

As with Italy, we think of Spain as being chock-full of its own charismatic local grape varieties, and it is, but Merlot has still pervaded its way through the red wine country of Spain with success. Like in Italy, it is used to soup up slightly wimpy red wines.

USA

Wherever Cabernet Sauvignon leads, Merlot follows. And vice versa, because one is yin to the other's yang – they make great blending partners. This means that Merlot is hugely important in California, where it is part of what is known as a Meritage blend. These wines must comprise at least two of these grapes: Cabernet Sauvignon, Merlot, Cabernet Franc, Malbec, Petit Verdot and Carmenère. They are big and rich and ripe, but with Merlot added to the mix, they're that little bit more approachable and ready for earlier drinking. But even when it's not blended with other grapes, Californian Merlot can be big, bold and rich.

In Washington State, the Merlots are generally less 'big' than those from California. They are fresher in style, but still have plenty of the grape's characteristic flavour traits, filled with black fruit, leather, aniseed and liquorice.

Australia

Australia seems to have left Merlot well alone, although (as we know) you will find it close to wherever Cabernet Sauvignon is grown, and in the true Australian style, when Merlot is a single-varietal wine, it will be ripe, plummy and juicy.

Did you know?
The grape variety Carmenère is actually what put Chilean 'Merlot' on the map. When Chilean Merlot started to become popular, much of it was actually made from Carmenère because the vines got mixed up in the vineyards.

 Taste Merlot's characteristic flavour traits: filled with black fruit, leather, aniseed and liquorice.

grenache & friends

Red Grenache makes some of the world's most serious wines and is also one of the world's most planted wine grapes, so it trades under several names: Grenache in France, Garnacha in Spain, Garnatxa in Basque country and Canonnau in Sardinia. Yet, it still doesn't have the international respect and adoration that other grapes enjoy. In an effort to raise awareness of its significance, in 2009 a bunch of diehard fanatics created International Grenache Day on the third Friday in September, to celebrate all things Grenache.

Why are fans getting noisy about Grenache? Well, partly because its plantings are sadly in decline, even though it is very important to some of the world's most significant wine hubs, like France, Spain and Italy, as well as the New World, Australia and California especially. It's bizarre that the plantings of Grenache are down, because the grape can produce fantastic red wines in environments that are hot and arid, so it functions – even better, it makes delicious wines – in a climate where other grapes would give up (and they may well give up in future as the Earth gets warmer). Grenache also has relatively low acidity, which is especially useful when it comes to pairing with food.

Sounds too good to be true? Well, Grenache is not without imperfections. You have to watch out for its alcohol level for a start, because it's a grape that ripens late, allowing the sugar levels (that convert to alcohol) to creep up. The grape's hang time on the vine can also increase the level of tannin, meaning Grenache-based wines need a little longer in the bottle before they are drunk.

As the title of this section suggests, Grenache is happiest when blended with other grapes, especially with Syrah/Shiraz and Mourvèdre, which is why you sometimes see GSM (Grenache, Syrah/Shiraz, Mourvèdre) on labels. Three of its best friends are Mourvèdre, Carignan and Cinsaut.

Mourvèdre/Monastrell/Mataro

This grape loves to be warm in the summer and not too cold in the winter, which is why it's never grown too far from the Mediterranean, although Australians like it in GSM too. It can be made as a varietal wine, one that's rich in fruit and bold in flavour. It adds three things to these wines: tannin thanks to its thick skin; a sweet and intense blackcurrant flavour; and finally, alcohol.

Carignan/Carignano/Cariñena/Mazuelo

Carignan isn't really in favour at the moment, and is often passed over for other grape varieties, even though it can be useful to add acidity and colour to red wine. It can also make some deliciously fragrant varietal wines, especially in the South of France where, at its best, Carignan grows on bush vines which are old, and this age adds complexity to the grape's flavour – so much so that 'bush vine' is now a familiar phrase on wine labels. Morocco and Israel are both Carignan-growing regions worth watching out for.

Cinsaut *Say it: san-so*

Cinsaut used to be very popular in South Africa and, in fact, it's one of the parents of the country's now flagship red grape, Pinotage (see page 62). Today, it's best known in France as part of blended red wines. It adds a floral, aromatic and plump, juicy quality to reds, but it also works well as a crunchily fresh, dry rosé.

grenache: regions, grapes & flavours

France

RHÔNE VALLEY This valley runs from Lyon to Avignon and is split in two on the winemaking map. While Syrah/Shiraz is the only red grape permitted in the northern Rhône (most people drop the 'Valley'), the southern Rhône red wines are all about blends.

CHÂTEAUNEUF-DU-PAPE, GIGONDAS, VACQUEYRAS & CÔTES DU RHÔNE ★

Grenache, Syrah/Shiraz, Mourvèdre, Cinsaut
Grenache rules in the southern Rhône, and especially in its most famous region, Châteauneuf-du-Pape, which produces bold, rich, earthy reds that need to be aged for a good few years, roughly eight, to be enjoyed at their best. Amazingly, Châteauneuf (the 'du-Pape' is often dropped) makes about as much wine as the whole of the northern Rhône put together, and is a wine region especially famous for its soil. It is covered with smooth boulders called *galets rouges*, that store heat well, and so produces riper grapes. Châteauneuf wines can be made from 18 different grapes, and each producer has its own magic recipe for the 'right' Châteauneuf that's rich in flavour, dark in colour and high in meaty tannins.

Gigondas, just north-east of Châteauneuf, makes wines that are comprised of up to 80% Grenache. Like Châteauneuf, these are wines that shouldn't be drunk early, and are usually at their peak when five to 10 years old. They're dark, rich, smooth, full of black fruits and peppery spice. You will find some nice, dry, punchy rosés made in Gigondas, too.

Vacqueyras is the newbie region. Nestled between Châteauneuf and Gigondas, it produces white, rosé and red wines, but really majors in red Grenache blends. They're big, herbal-flavoured wines, with lots of black plum fruit, and often black pepper notes because Syrah/Shiraz is Grenache's main partner here.

Côtes du Rhône is a regional category for wines that span the Rhône Valley. It is one of those prolific names on restaurant wine lists because it's very versatile with food. Côtes du Rhône-Villages is its superior, and indicates a minimum of 40% Grenache content. They're full of juicy plum and blackcurrant fruit, and are designed for drinking relatively early. They are sumptuous and very drinkable red wines.

LANGUEDOC-ROUSSILLON ★

Grenache, Syrah/Shiraz, Mourvèdre, Carignan
These juicy red wines have improved enormously in the last 20 years. Syrah/Shiraz wears the crown in terms of importance, but Grenache is also a big deal. Producers in this region are experimental with their wines, and a Languedoc-Roussillon blend is often my go-to choice of red in a restaurant. The best Grenache blends not only have deep, black fruit with gentle tannins, but they capture the woody herbs of the area, too, especially thyme. Regions worth looking out for are Côtes Catalanes, Corbiéres, Faugères, Fitou, Minervois and Saint-Chinian.

TAVEL Grenache is hugely important in Tavel, mostly for its spicy and serious dry rosé (see pages 66–69).

Did you know?
You can also get white Châteauneuf-du-Pape. It's not as common as the red, but it's growing in popularity, and can be made from any of the following grapes: Grenache Blanc, Clairette, Roussanne, Bourboulenc and Picardan.

Spain
RIOJA & NAVARRA
Garnacha, Tempranillo

Garnacha is incredibly important in Spain's most famous wine region, Rioja. It plays a lead (but not the leading) role alongside Tempranillo (see pages 50–53) as the framework of most red Rioja. Loved for their rich, red-fruit flavours, white-pepper spice, and herbal and spicy notes; you can also taste vanilla and chocolate. Garnacha is especially important in Rioja Baja, the easternmost of the three Rioja sub-regions, furthest from the sea, where it is hotter. Next door to Rioja, Navarra does a good job at making red wines that are similar to red Rioja in style, but at a slightly lower price. Navarra, however, is really known for its Grenache-filled *rosado* (rosé) wines (see pages 66–69).

PRIORAT
Cariñena, Garnacha, Syrah/Shiraz

A relatively recent success, this Catalonian region, south-west of Barcelona, is a great story of a wine region being revived. It's a super-swanky winemaking area that is the only Spanish region other than Rioja to be awarded the highest wine classification (DOCa). Here, Garnacha is best when blended with Cariñena, and a lot of praise is awarded to the unique slate soil, called llicorella (*say it: yickor-ey-a*). Red wines from Priorat are dense with ripe black fruit, but also have a liquorice spice and often a fair dose of chocolate, too. They command a pretty big price and are not meant to be drunk early. Give them at least eight years to mellow.

Italy
Cannonau, Carignano

Sardinia is the only stronghold of Cannonau (Grenache) in Italy, and some people even think it's the birthplace of the variety. This is one of the places where you can find 100% Cannonau, made into dry or sweet wines, or blended with Carignano. The dry wines are big, beefy, even jammy in flavour, and given the heat on the island, it's hardly surprising that these wines often reach alcohol levels of 15% ABV (alcohol by volume). If you're having a barbecue, a big and rustic Cannonau di Sardegna is just the wine you need.

USA

In both California and Washington, rich, spicy and generous Grenache-blended cult wines are popping up. These are far more interesting than any of the very cheap Grenache found in California. The better-quality blends in both states are rich in black cherry and have a lovely liquorice spice. Think Châteauneuf, but bigger!

Australia
Grenache, Shiraz, Mataro

Grenache is hot property in Australia right now. And so it should be, because Grenache's love of hot and arid conditions makes Australia a no-brainer of a place to make it. Again, it is shown at its best when blended with other grapes, especially Shiraz and Mataro – the Australians are big fans of that acronym GSM. South Australia is where Grenache and its blending friends rule, and I'd earmark McLaren Vale, Barossa Valley and Langhorne Creek as regions with intense GSM wines.

Israel
Grenache, Syrah/Shiraz, Mourvèdre, Carignan

There's a slow but exciting change happening here. Many quality-conscious Israeli producers now see the potential in Grenache and friends which are often more suited to Israeli conditions than Bordeaux grapes. They're rich and meaty wines with a smoky spice.

spanish reds

People who choose nothing but Rioja for their Spanish red wine fix are missing a trick. Not that there's anything wrong with Rioja, of course, but it's a shame to pigeonhole a country as having one decent red wine when it has so much more to offer. Spain, like other Old World countries, has upped its game in recent years. It still makes masses of wine, and some of it can be pretty mediocre, but just as with Italy, these days there's more of a focus on quality rather than quantity - a welcome move in any wine-lover's book.

The modern improvement in quality of Spanish red wines has involved a few things: tweaking grape blends (but not beyond the point of recognition), championing forgotten grape varieties and regions that have great potential, as well as adopting new techniques to make red wines more thoughtfully, rather than just, say, throwing loads of oak at them.

There's also a more thoughtful approach to vine planting. For Spain, this is really about altitude, because across much of Spain, the ground temperature is just too hot to grow good grapes for wine. So today, vines are increasingly found at higher altitudes where it's cooler, and this usually means the wines both taste fresher and will be lower in alcohol.

Tempranillo *Say it: temp-ra-knee-oh*

Tempranillo is the backbone red wine grape in Spain, and although it's also important as Tinta Roriz in Portugal, it is now one of the popular red grapes being produced in New World winemaking hot spots.

Tempranillo loves hot and arid conditions. It soaks up the heat without necessarily accumulating too much sugar, which means it doesn't always reach the same alcohol heights as Garnacha (see pages 46–49). In general, Tempranillo's flavour is more about leather and spice than the bucket loads of fruit like in Garnacha and other red grapes. The earthy flavours can be gorgeously plush, and because Tempranillo doesn't have loads of natural acidity, it often makes wines that are mellow rather than fresh. If producers want to perk up the acidity in Tempranillo, they'll

simply blend it with another grape – it's very cooperative, and is happy being blended.

It used to be possible to pick Spanish Tempranillo out in a crowd thanks to the American oak barrels, which gave the wines a trademark vanilla flavour. Today, it's not so easy to spot for several reasons: there's increasingly more Tempranillo grown around the world; wines from Spanish regions other than Rioja are now more available to us; and the use of oak in Tempranillo has changed – French oak is used more often now, plus it spends significantly less time ageing in oak than it used to in any case.

RIOJA

It might be in northern central Spain – or if you're a foodie – due south of San Sebastián, but Rioja is the epicentre of Spanish red wine for many people, and Tempranillo plays the leading role. As a region, Rioja really hit the big time in terms of being an acceptable

---

Regional namesakes

Remember, in Spain, like the rest of Europe, the region where wine is made often gives the name to the wine style, too, rather than the grape varieties from which the wine is made. For example, Rioja, Ribera del Duero, Toro, Navarra…

spanish reds:
grapes, regions & flavours

and revered wine in the 1970s. Since then, it's been on a bit of a rollercoaster ride with its style. In the '80s and '90s there was a bigger emphasis on quality rather than quantity, more French barrels were used and Tempranillo spent less time in oak. These two changes in winemaking techniques are what those in the industry refer to as 'modern Rioja', but that doesn't necessarily mean they're better wines.

Today, the region is changing again, as producers try to re-authenticate red Rioja by highlighting its unique identity. This in part means returning to some of the older methods, albeit with a modern twist. Whether it's modern or not, Tempranillo shines through in red Rioja as a smooth and supple wine with flavours of leather and tobacco.

Tempranillo is grown in all three of Rioja's sub-regions: Alta, Alavesa and Baja, although Baja is the easternmost and hottest sub-region so Garnacha is more common there (see pages 46–49). Tempranillo makes up about two-thirds of Rioja's vineyards but it's often blended with other grapes, the most common being Garnacha, but Mazuelo and Monastrell are also important.

Not all Tempranillo is made in Spain...
Tempranillo thrives in places that can withstand hot conditions. This means places like Portugal, America and Australia can make fantastic Tempranillo. In Portugal, it is called 'Tinta Roriz' or 'Aragonez' (or 'Aragonês'), depending on where it's made.

NAVARRA
Just like its neighbour Rioja, Tempranillo is important in blended red wines here, although it's nowhere near as important to the region as Garnacha. Still, they make wines that aren't too dissimilar to red Rioja, with that leather, spice and tobacco flavour, but they're generally slightly lighter in style.

CATALONIA
Tempranillo is one of the most important varieties across all of Catalonia's sub-regions, although many parts of this area are embracing 'international' grapes like Cabernet Sauvignon, too.

VALDEPEÑAS
The baking heat of southern central Spain has seen a revival of red wines recently, and Tempranillo, known locally as Cencibel, is making some smooth and smoky reds without being heavy or serious. It's still early days here, but definitely an area to keep an eye on.

RIBERA DEL DUERO
This is where Spanish wine got modern. Ribera del Duero (often shortened to 'Ribera') is the region that climbed the social wine echelons quickly in the 1990s. And that's all thanks to Tempranillo, which doesn't just have one name here, but two: Tinto Fino and Tinto del País.

Excitingly different to red Rioja, the Tempranillo in Ribera makes wines that are fruitier than Rioja, not in a sappy-fruit way, but in a deep, intense and concentrated way – a way that makes you sit up and take notice. This is not only because of the extra fruit, but because they usually taste more lively and pretty fresh, too, for Tempranillo. Ribera is further inland than Rioja and more continental, with cooler nights allowing the grape's flavour to develop slowly. These wines are capable of extended ageing – the best ones aren't ready until they're at least 10 years old.

Producers to look out for are Torres with their Ribera wine Celeste, Abadía Retuerta, Pesquera and finally Vega Sicilia, which is Spain's most iconic winery and makes a cult wine. Vega Sicilia's wines are made from Tempranillo and are typically blended with grapes that are famous in Bordeaux, like Cabernet Sauvignon and Merlot. Unico is the top Vega Sicilia wine and reaches a hefty price. It's mostly Tempranillo, and isn't usually released until 10 years after it's made.

CIGALES

A hot and dry region, but not so much as its neighbour Ribera. These two regions share the local name for Tempranillo, Tinta del País. Cigales makes tighter, fresher red wines than its famous neighbour, but so far its most acclaimed wines are pink rather than red.

Bobal

Spain's secondmost planted red grape hasn't made any headlines internationally yet, but that could soon change because the wine community is getting a bit frisky about it. It has a bit of a bad-kid-come-good history because in the past, Bobal was a popular grape for bulk wine production, but now there's more thoughtful planting of the vines at higher altitudes, which gives extra freshness to the wines. The best of this new breed of Bobals make reds that taste of plums, but the masterstroke is their smooth and supple character combined with decent acidity, all of which make them very good drinking wines rather than wines for keeping. It is this chirpy, fruity character that sees Bobal increasingly made into pink wine, too.

Mostly, Bobal is found in the regions that head out from the heart of central Spain towards Valencia, such as Manchuela, Utiel Requena and the winemaking area named Valencia (not to be confused with the city). Try the Bobal from Bodegas y Viñedos Ponce, if you can.

Mencía *Say it: menth-eeya* ★

If I were allowed to have a favourite Spanish red grape, this would probably be it (at the moment anyway) because it makes red wines with attitude and doesn't need to be slathered in oak or blended with other varieties to prove itself. Grown in north-west Spain, Mencía can make ripe and fruity reds as well as firm and serious ones, but whichever style it is, they're both seriously delicious.

Some of the regions where this grape is best known include Ribeira Sacra, Monterrei and Valdeorras, where you can also find the lovely white Godello grape. The most exciting Mencía hotspot, though, is the region of Bierzo, which borders Valdeorras. This is where the floral bouquet of Mencía and pretty, perky juicy beetroot/beet flavour is captured at its best. Palacios, which is a producer name more familiar in Priorat (see page 49), invested in Bierzo and makes some truly great wines. While Pena das Donas and Raúl Pérez are lesser-known names, they also make fantastic Mencía.

Graciano

This is increasing in popularity and peps up a wine with its floral aroma and fresh acidity. It also has good tannins, so it's a useful grape to help a Rioja age well.

International grapes

It's not completely unheard of to find international grapes in Spanish reds, including some Cabernet Sauvignon skulking around in Rioja's vineyards.

italian reds

If you're looking for wines that reek of authenticity and flavour, look no further than Italy. While I'm objective in my work, in my downtime there's no question that I have a huge personal interest in Italian wine. In fact, last Christmas, my entire day's drinking consisted of Italian wine; from fizz at the start of the day through to sticky wine at the end. This chapter pays homage to Italian reds, and there's no shortage of wines to pay homage to. One of the beautiful things about Italian wines is all those inimitable local grape varieties, which make this country a hive of delicious, distinctive red wines.

Nebbiolo ★
BAROLO & BARBARESCO, PIEDMONT

One of the jewels in Italy's crown, Nebbiolo, makes mesmerizing red wines. Its trademark character is the powerful aroma, which is like crushing black peppercorns in a pestle and mortar, then squishing in a few sour black cherries. Its home is in the north-east, Piedmont. Here it makes hedonistic red wines in the villages of Barolo and Barbaresco (which are also names of wine styles). Barolo is thought to be more meaty and masculine, whereas Barbaresco is prettier and feminine. Both styles are high in tannin, so in my experience, they should never be drunk very young, and can take as long as a decade to soften enough to enjoy. But they're so gorgeous we're probably all a bit guilty of drinking them too young.

Want younger-drinking Nebbiolo?
Nebbiolo doesn't just make wines that age for decades. A wine termed 'Langhe Nebbiolo' offers delicious Nebbiolo character, but it's one that's designed for younger drinking. Also, for all its brilliance, Nebbiolo has yet to be cracked by any country other than Italy, and in fact it's rarely seen outside of Piedmont.

Barbera
PIEDMONT

Another red grape that's local, and special, to Piedmont, even though you can find it in other pockets of Italy. Small pockets. Barbera usually gives its name to the regions where it's grown, the most popular being Barbera d'Asti and Barbera d'Alba. Of these two, Barbera is more of a speciality in the region of Asti, but it's Barbera d'Alba that usually costs more. A bit like Nebbiolo, Barbera can cross the boundaries from being an easy-drinking red with dense, cherry flavours and softer raspberry flavours, to a big, dark and rich wine. Conterno and Fantino make some truly gorgeous Barbera wines.

Sangiovese *Say it: sanjo-vair-zee*
CHIANTI, TUSCANY &... EVERYWHERE

Sangiovese, or derivations of it (this grape mutates at the drop of a hat) can be found all over Italy. But it's most famous and most revered in Tuscany, especially in Chianti, which is a sub-region within Tuscany, as well as the name of its wine style, of course.

Chianti is split further into sub-regions, and of these Chianti Classico is widely recognized as the highest-quality, and will therefore usually cost more than a wine that's labelled simply as 'Chianti'. These wines can be very good value for money, but it can also be a bit of a gamble, because people feel safe choosing the brand Chianti, so some wines can get away with being not quite as good as they should be.

italian reds:
grapes, regions & flavours

Chiantis, when good, are full of cherry fruit and often have a delicious aroma of tomatoes and oregano. They can be quite versatile with food, too, so are popular on restaurant wine lists, especially because the Chianti brand recognition is very strong around the world.

Brunello
MONTALCINO, TUSCANY

Remember I talked about Sangiovese mutating? Brunello is the perfect case in point. Montalcino is also in Tuscany and its Brunello di Montalcino wines are a bit like Sangiovese Chiantis on steroids. They're bigger and meatier with strong tannins when the wines are young, so you need to give them a few years to smooth out. Want a cheaper, younger-drinking red from this region? Try a Rosso di Montalcino.

Montepulciano
ABRUZZO

Another popular name, Montepulciano d'Abruzzo is a juicy red wine without too much tannin and lots of cherry fruit. It's a no-brainer red for wine lists, although it's hardly ever a wine to keep for ageing.

Primitivo
PUGLIA

Primitivo is a grape that has a super-dark colour and becomes a wine that's full of liquorice spice and very thick, concentrated cherry flavours. It's unashamedly full-on and packed with flavour. But be careful; it can be quite high in alcohol. I once heard a winemaker say, 'If Primitivo is less than 15% ABV (alcohol by volume) it isn't evenly balanced' – I wouldn't necessarily agree, but be warned!

Nero d'Avola & Nerello Mascalese 👁 ★
SICILY

Nero d'Avola is a grape that's largely used in the making of everyday-drinking wines. It's good on its own, and brings lots of big, fresh, black-fruit flavour to the party, with an extra-dry kick of cumin and paprika.

Nerello Mascalese is the new kid on the block. Its arrival on the world stage is a fairly recent one, but it hasn't taken long to show everyone the quality of the wines it can make, elevating Sicily's position from its high-volume, low-quality image of the past. The grape name isn't always displayed, but if a wine says 'Etna Rosso', you can be pretty sure it will have a large dollop of Nerello Mascalese in the mix. It is also often blended with its lesser-quality sibling, Nerello Cappuccio. Etna Rossos have lovely, soft raspberry flavours and are like a cross between Nebbiolo and Pinot Noir.

Feminine & masculine wines

Some people balk at the idea of calling wines masculine or feminine, but to me, this is political correctness gone mad, because it's a widely understood and helpful way of encapsulating a wine's character. For example, Barolo is universally recognized as the masculine interpretation of Nebbiolo, while Barbaresco is the more feminine style. Easy, right?

'Super Tuscans'

A quick bit of history here, because Super Tuscans are the exception to the Italian wine rule. Back in the 1960s, a bunch of producers boldly started making top-end wine from grapes that were not local to the region – international grapes like Cabernet Sauvignon and Merlot. This meant that no matter how good the wines were, they weren't eligible to attain the DOCG status – the highest quality category in Italy. This didn't matter to these pioneering producers, though, and rather than people thinking they were lesser-quality, their fame and adoration only grew because of their notoriety. Famous Super Tuscan names include Sassicaia, Ornellaia and Tignanello, and these wines are rich and dense, and do a brilliant job of being both identifiable as Cabernet Sauvignon and Merlot, but also of honing the slickness of Italy. These wines are iconic and made in small volume – in other words, they're never cheap.

Corvina, Molinara & Rondinella
VENETO

Veneto's most famous wine, Valpolicella, is a refreshing red wine that's frisky, full of cherries and has an unusual twist of marzipan to it. It's made from a blend of local grapes, Corvina, Molinara and Rondinella. Corvina is usually thought of as being the best quality, as well as the most important of these grapes, so it is always the most prominent.

Amarone di Valpolicella, usually shortened to just 'Amarone', is made in a slightly different way – the grapes are left to shrivel up and dehydrate, so the sugars concentrate inside the grape. This often means the wine tastes more concentrated than other Valpolicellas, replacing the cherry flavour with that of raisin. The increase in sugar also means this wine has higher alcohol levels. In fact, the law stipulates that Amarone must be a minimum of 14% ABV.

In Italy, as in other European countries, it is often the region where a wine is produced that lends its name to a wine style, as opposed to the name of the prominent grape. Some use both, like the Barberas, Barbera d'Asti and Barbera d'Alba. This is less true of Italian white wine styles, where the names principally highlight the grapes and occasionally add on the region. Here are a few names to watch out for, alongside the grapes used to make them to help you recognize what's what in Italian wines.

ITALIAN REGIONS THAT GIVE NAMES TO RED WINE STYLES

Region & style	Grape
Barolo	Nebbiolo
Barbaresco	Nebbiolo
Chianti	Sangiovese
Etna (Rosso)	Nerello Mascalese, Nerello Cappuccio
Valpolicella	Corvina, Molinara, Rondinella

malbec

concentrated

perfumed

spicy

creamy

earthy

meaty

The original name for Malbec – Cot, sometimes Côt – has never caught on, even though it's not exactly difficult to say. But no matter what you call it, we can't seem to get enough of this grape at the moment, thanks to its chunky handsomeness and lashings of blackcurrant fruit.

Known for being a no-brainer pairing with steak, Malbec makes rich and juicy dark-red wines wherever it is produced. Although it's most famous as a varietal wine (made on its own rather than blended with other grapes) it isn't unusual to blend Malbec. Especially so in its natural home, Cahors in south-west France, where it's known as Cot or Auxerrois.

🏠 Cahors, France

Widely believed to be the home of this grape, wines in this region must be made from at least 70% Cot, while Merlot or Tannat make up the rest of the blend. If producers don't adhere to this rule they can't put the Cahors name on the label, and they definitely don't want to miss out on that, because Cahors wines are held in high esteem, commanding some of the greatest respect of all the wines made in south-west France.

When it comes to style, Cahors wines can be more rustic and earthy in flavour than the Malbecs you fine in the southern hemisphere. They are delicious with any dish where red meat and big flavour play leading roles.

Did you know?
Malbec is wonderful as a rich red, but also delicious in pink wine, because it's easy to extract lots of colour and flavour from its berries and skin.

This grape...
SMELLS:
floral · leathery ·
perfumed · smoky ·
spicy · toasty
TASTES OF:
black olive · black
pepper · blackcurrant ·
cherry · chocolate ·
cinnamon · liquorice ·
plum · raspberry ·
truffle

malbec: **regions & flavours**

Argentina

Bright, pure, full of juicy, black fruit and with creamy oak flavours – this is Argentinian Malbec in a nutshell. In fact, Malbec has been so successful in Argentina, it can now be found all over South America, from Chile to Peru. But Argentina remains the unequivocal daddy of southern hemisphere Malbec and, particularly its region of Mendoza. To go even further, we can hone in on Mendoza's sub-region, the Uco Valley, which is fast becoming a superior Malbec Mecca. So superior, in fact, that 'Uco Valley' or 'Valle de Uco' is often proudly displayed on the bottle labels – look out for it.

Malbec has such a long history in Argentinian soil that its growers are at a distinct advantage when it comes to selecting the best fields and vines. The vineyards are at high altitudes in a hot climate, which is perfect for Malbec, and the growing season is long, meaning there are plenty of good-quality grapes.

When Malbec hit the big time in Argentina, it was mostly for single-varietal (made purely from this grape variety) Malbecs. But there's a growing trend towards making wines that are based on Malbec, with other grapes thrown in, like Cabernet Sauvignon and Merlot, all in the name of elevating the wine's complexity. Some of my favourite producers of pure Malbec include Pulenta and Achaval Ferrer.

USA

Malbec is grown all over the United States, but it's most popular in California and Washington State. In California, it's often used to beef up red blends, while in Washington, it makes elegant, black-fruited wines. As in Argentina, Washington has a long growing season but when it gets very hot, very quickly, it can lead to grapes that are high in sugar but with less depth of flavour than their Argentinian cousins.

Chile

The first Chilean Malbec I tasted blew me away. It was made by a French winemaker and the fruit came from Casablanca Valley, the region that put Chile on the map in terms of making serious white wines. Today, the number of people making Malbec in Chile is on the up, and not just from Casablanca, either, but from vineyards all over the country. I often find Chilean Malbecs to be less full-bodied than those from Argentina, but they have an extra kick of black-pepper spice, which is very refreshing.

Australia

As Australia endeavours to show that it's more than just a one-trick pony (that trick being Shiraz, see pages 32–35), we'll see more Malbec coming out of Australia in years to come. Of course Malbec and Shiraz both make big, rich, fruity wines, but from what I've tasted so far, the Australian ones, especially those from Margaret River in western Australia and Langhorne Creek in southern Australia, are worth checking out.

flagship reds

As well as all of the other red wine styles featured in this book there are some benchmark grapes that certain regions champion to make their flagship styles of wine. Here, I take a look at some of the most important grapes in their flagship 'homes'.

Zinfandel
CALIFORNIA

Discussing Zinfandel's origin and parentage is a bit like watching 'The Jerry Springer Show'. There have been claims, counter-claims, confusion and disagreements. Now, it's conclusive, and it didn't even need a lie detector test to prove it. Zinfandel is the same grape as Primitivo in Puglia, but it actually hails from the Croatian Dalmatian Coast.

But Zinfandel is famous for more than just disputes. In California, it's taken rosé to a new level. White Zinfandel or Zinfandel Blush is an incredible pink wine success – it's also largely responsible for the idea that all rosés are sweet.

As a dry red wine, Zinfandel is taken much more seriously. And it's a whopper, too. In fact Ravenswood, a much-respected producer of Zinfandel in California, uses the tag line 'No Wimpy Wines', which gives you an idea of its power and strength. Usually a combination of spicy red fruit with leather and liquorice, good red 'Zin' producers include Ravenswood, Seghesio and Turley.

Pinotage
SOUTH AFRICA

A divisive grape that's often referred to as South Africa's flagship red. It was created in Stellenbosch in the early 20th century and is a cross of Pinot Noir with Cinsaut (South Africans used to call Cinsaut 'Hermitage', hence the hybrid name). Pinotage makes macho wines that are meaty, rich, smoky and really quite tannic. They are barbecue wines that work well with grilled red meat.

It's divisive because it has a tendency to taste of things like burnt rubber. However, the general quality of Pinotage has improved in recent years, and in fact, when I was last in South Africa I tasted several really good styles – the best I'd ever tasted. They just don't seem to get exported much. If you can get hold of them, try the Pinotages from Rijk's, Bellingham and Groot Constantia.

Most recently, and controversially, red Pinotage has been seasoned with a very deliberate coffee or chocolate flavour (achieved through oak), giving producers the opportunity to give names to their wines like Barista and Cuppapinoccinotage.

Carmenère *Say it: carmenair*
CHILE

Never has a case of mistaken wine identity been more famous than that of Carmenère in Chile, where for years it was accidentally confused and identified as Merlot. What's bizarre is that, even though the Chilean wine boom happened on the back of 'Merlot', today people continue to drink it, except now it actually is Merlot, and not Carmenère. If you've been a Chilean Merlot fan from day one, but have been disappointed in recent years, this might explain why.

Carmenère actually comes from Bordeaux, although it's hardly used there these days. In its newest adopted land it makes some fantastically rich and flavoursome red wines. Depending on the heat of the area in which it's grown, its flavours can range from having a herbal-green flavour of black fruit to spicy chocolate at its richest. Names to look out for include De Martino and Marques de Casa Concha.

Gamay
BEAUJOLAIS, FRANCE

Make way for Gamay in your wine rack or fridge – this grape makes one of the most versatile wines around: Beaujolais. Beaujolais can be so juicy it's practically bursting out of your mouth, or it can be earthy and savoury.

Like many other French regions there is a quality hierarchy in Beaujolais. In its most basic form, Beaujolais (the wine style) can be a sappy, red-fruited wine that needs to be drunk within one year. Beaujolais-Villages is a step up in quality and can be kept for longer, say three to four years – these are often really good value for money. Cru Beaujolais lists the names of the crus (the 10 villages in the region that produce the highest-quality Gamay) on the label, including Brouilly and Fleurie, Juliénas, Morgon and Moulin-à-Vent. These wines can get pretty serious, and can even age by as much as 10 years, although I think they're often at their best when they're five to eight years old. 'Beaujolais Nouveau' is a special term given to a Beaujolais that's released in the November of each year, very soon after the wine has been made. These are unoaked, so are very light and fruity wines.

The freshness, upfront fruit and lack of heavy tannin in Beaujolais make it a hugely food-friendly wine. Good producers include Henry Fessy, Jean-Paul Thévenet, Château Grange Cochard and Domaine de Prion.

SWITZERLAND

Gamay is very popular in the French-speaking part of Switzerland and Pinot Noir rules in German-speaking Switzerland. Sometimes these two grapes are even blended, especially in wines from Dôle. Wherever it's made, the cool conditions of Switzerland mean that its Gamay gives a pure, fragrant and raspberry-flavoured wine which makes for supple, easy drinking.

Tannat
URUGUAY

Uruguay is not technically the 'home' of this grape, but it has adopted it as its signature style. Tannat was brought to Uruguay by a Frenchman, and as the name suggests, it makes pretty tannic wines, plus they often have good acidity. Both are attributes that a wine needs to age well, although I've yet to taste any old ones to prove this. Tannat's home is actually Madiran in south-west France, and wow, does that region make some delicious, mineral, fresh but ballsy red wines! But, if you compare the tannins of wines made from Tannat in Madiran to those in Uruguay, you'll generally see a softer side to the South American wines, thanks to the warmer climate. The best Uruguayan Tannats really need plenty of fruit to show through beyond the grip of tannin and freshness of acidity in the mouth. De Lucca and Juanicó are two great producers.

Blaufränkisch *Say it: blauw-fran-kish* ★
AUSTRIA

There's a real buzz in the air surrounding Austria's

Why is Beaujolais so juicy?

The Gamay in Beaujolais doesn't just achieve serious levels of fruitiness because of the grape; it's boosted by a method of fermentation that produces wines that are meant to be drunk early. This is called 'carbonic maceration'. It involves the fermentation of the grape juice inside each individual grape, which is different to the traditional method of fermentation, where grapes are crushed to release the juice and then all the juice ferments in a big tank.

flagship red grape at the moment. Although I call it the flagship red grape, another red grape called Zweigelt is actually the most planted in Austria. The style of Blaufränkisch has changed for the better since the mid-1980s, when producers threw loads of oak at the grape, stopping its flavours from shining through. Today, the use of oak on Blaufränkisch is much more sensitive, meaning it can finally show its 'sense of place'; its character. A very refreshing red wine without being aggressive in acidity, it stays fresh even in warmer years, plus it has many, many food-matching possibilities. I think Blaufränkisch is delicious when it's just a few years old, but many producers think it tastes at its best several years after it's made. It isn't a cheap wine to make, so you won't find any budget bottles on the shelves, but it's worth the money, especially those from Wachter-Wiesler, Triebaumer, Umathum and Heinrich Gernot & Keike.

Touriga Nacional *Say it: tooreegah nass-ion-ahl*
PORTUGAL

After years of quietly plugging away as one of the most important red grapes for Port, Touriga Nacional has been thrust into the limelight over the last 10 years as the backbone of some of Portugal's finest red wines. Touriga Nacional usually needs to be fleshed out with another Portuguese native red grape, like Tinta Cão or Touriga Franca, but it's still the main reason why these dark and rich red wines have such an attractive pure, blackcurrant, floral aroma. They're bold and rich reds with very distinctive characters, especially from producers Wine & Soul, Quinta do Noval and Quinta do Vale Maria.

Plavac Mali *Say it: plavatz mahlee*
CROATIA

Plavac Mali loves, loves, loves the heat, although it's made in central and southern Dalmatia, as well as on the islands. The best wines are made from grapes grown on the southern Kras slopes, where they're in full view of the sun. These can make big and tannic wines, and they're not shy on alcohol, either; sometimes they can reach as much as (gulp) 16% ABV (alcohol by volume). As a big red wine, though, they can be delicious and intense, and there's an attractive distinctive quality to this grape. It smells of dried herbs and dried flowers, while in the mouth it's very rich and often tastes of figs and prunes as well as chocolate and vanilla.

Agiorgitiko *Say it: ah-your-yee-te-koh*
GREECE

Greece's most widely planted red makes every kind of wine, from funky, fruity rosé to deep-flavoured and serious reds that are worth ageing. It's best as a red wine that's rich and spicy, and tastes of currants and liquorice. It's most famously made in the Peloponnese district of Nemea, where the producer Gaia is one of the finest.

rosé

The world is ablaze with a love of pink wine at the moment, so much so that people are starting to take it seriously rather than dismiss it as some frivolous girly drink. Even so, it's worth remembering how few pricey rosés are out there on the shelves – unless it's Champagne, of course. Rosé is a versatile wine for all sorts of reasons. Sure, it can be the quaffable, thirst-quenching, fruity summer drink, but it's also fantastic with food, and quite a wide range of foods at that. I've listed them by style here as it's the best way to identify rosé.

Rosés can be made anywhere that red wines are made, because the colour comes from the skin of red grapes. The pulp (and therefore juice) of all grapes is colourless, which explains why you can make white wines from red grapes, as long as you separate the skins quickly enough. The colour of the pink varies hugely, from pale to dark and from onion-skin (as people in the wine trade say) to the colour of pomegranate seeds. The differences in colour depend on the grapes used and the length of maceration time (see below).

There are three ways to add colour to rosé: maceration, saignée and blending. Maceration keeps the pulp (juice) of the grape in contact with the skin of the grape, so it draws out colour. The longer this takes place, the darker the wine colour. Saignée is French for 'bled', and as a red wine starts to ferment, some of the wine will be 'bled' off into another container so the contact of the juice with the skins is shorter, making the wine pink rather than red. This method generally makes rich rosés. Finally, blending involves adding a little red wine to white wine. This is illegal in many places and is most widely done in Champagne, where it is legal.

Dry & elegant ★
PROVENCE, FRANCE
Ahh… the engine room of some of the world's most delicious rosés. This is as serious as rosé can get, and as far as I can see local varieties such as Syrah,

Grenache, Carignan and Cinsaut are to thank for the melting pot of tasty rosés from Provence. They're refreshing and bursting with floral, sweet, red apple and crunchy pomegranate fruit flavours, so they're a match made in heaven with the garlic and aioli-influenced food of the region. If you want to go swanky and serious with Provençal rosé, try the wines at Domaine Ott, and if you want something a bit more affordable and organic, Château Léoube is a great producer, but I'm also a fan of the wines at Domaine Sainte Lucie, which has a great brand called MiP (Made in Provence).

Dry or off-dry & elegant
LOIRE VALLEY, FRANCE
There are some lovely, pretty rosés from the Loire Valley, usually made from Cabernet Franc or Pinot Noir. They're delicate, zesty and can sometimes have a little hit of extra sweetness, so small that you'd hardly notice, but enough to make them a great match with a

You say rosé
Rosé is such a familiar wine name that it's universally used for pink wines, even if it isn't the right word in the wine's local language.

dish that has some spice to it. The dry ones are always excellent with seafood.

Dry or off-dry & fruity
PORTUGAL

Some of my favourite rosés, or *rosados* as the Portuguese say, come from Portugal. This country's local dark-skinned grapes have an abundance of natural flavour and colour, so it only stands to reason they'd work well as pink wines, too. In the Douro Valley, Touriga Nacional – which is the most famous grape in Port production – is making brilliant dry and perky pink wines. They often taste of pomegranate to me, although the best styles also have a sour, grapefruit freshness. Speaking of Port, even that has got in on the rosé action now. Pink Port was created by the Port house Taylor's in 2010, and is so successful many other houses now make it, too. It's especially good as a base for cocktails. Other Portuguese rosado regions worth looking out for are Vinho Verde and Alentejo.

Dry or off-dry, fruity & spicy
SOUTH OF THE EQUATOR

Generous sunshine hours make red grapes ripen easily, so countries like Chile, Argentina, South Africa, New Zealand and Australia can make some belter rosés, full of crunchy red fruits. They're sunshine in the bottle, and are made to be drunk in the sun, too! Typically, they're made with grapes that are best known within each country. In Chile, Cabernet Sauvignon, Merlot and Carmenère make deep-coloured rosés with lots of grip to the bright, juicy-fruit flavour. In Argentina, it's Malbec. The colour is deep, it tastes bold and fruity, and it loves Argentinian prawn/shrimp ceviche. In Australia, Shiraz and Cabernet Sauvignon make deep-coloured rosés with a good bite of black-pepper spice. Mostly dry, sometimes they're off-dry, too. In New Zealand, the grape used varies by region. It could be Merlot, Pinot Noir or Syrah/Shiraz but they're

Like it sweet?
If you prefer sweeter rosés, anything with the following phrases on the label will probably be sweeter in style: White Merlot, White Zinfandel, Zinfandel Blush or Pink Moscato.

usually bright pink in colour, very fruity and dry. In South Africa, Pinotage rosés often have a smoky edge to their fruit, making them good for barbecues, and usually they're dry.

Dry, bold & fruity
NAVARRA, SPAIN

Many Spanish regions make *rosado*, of course, but Navarra is especially good for rich and handsome styles with bucket loads of flavour and attitude. Usually, they're made from Garnacha and are deep pink in colour. Most of them are dry, and they have an upfront, juicy style with crushed-strawberry flavour.

PUGLIA, ITALY

Rosato, as the Italians call rosé, is made all over Italy, from the north-west corner of Piedmont to the heel in Puglia. Down in Puglia, in the sub-region of Salice Salentino, some lovely rosatos are made with plenty of rich colour, cherry-flavoured fruit and a zesty spice – they're great with tomato-based food.

NAPA VALLEY, CALIFORNIA, USA

For drier rosés than the generic Californian style, take a look at those made in Napa with Cabernet Sauvignon. California's crown jewel of Cabernet Sauvignon production makes deep-coloured rosés with a richness of fruit that is so intense, if you tasted them blind you might even think you were drinking red wine.

Medium & fruity
CALIFORNIA, USA

You can't deny it; Zinfandel Blush or White Zinfandel is a pink wine craze. People love the sweeter style that tastes of confectionery, and these wines are impossible to ignore on the shelf because the colour is almost neon. Although I'm sure many people drink it by itself, or on the rocks, these rosés can also work with red fruit desserts like a strawberry tart.

Dry & very light
FRIULI, ITALY

Check out Pinot Grigio Ramato if you like light rosé. You see, Pinot Grigio has a slight pink tinge to its skin, and sometimes this comes through in the wine, giving a very light copper colour that's enough to squeeze it into this rosé section. Pinot Grigio Ramatos are very different to the Pinot Grigios most of us know, and have a lightly chewy texture and a gentle apple flavour.

Pink fizz

Everywhere that makes sparkling wine usually makes a sparkling rosé, too. These are typically fruitier versions of the white sparkling wines from each region because the juice has spent more time leaking flavour and colour from the red grapes. This means places such as England that have a cool climate are especially proud of their sparkling rosé wines because the red fruit gives them an extra layer of flavour. Speaking of which, I really like the rosé from Gusbourne, Coates & Seely, Jenkyn Place and Digby Fine English. Rosé Champagnes also offer serious depth of flavour, enough to be able to pair them with meat dishes. I'm a huge fan of those made by Charles Heidsieck, Bollinger and Dosnon & Lepage.

Rosé & food

I'm totally into dry rosé with food – it's really versatile so there are many options.

Food coming off a griddle has that extra-smoky flavour, which means a robust (probably southern hemisphere) rosé is a great option to pair with barbecue food. These should also have enough guts to match the richness of, say, sausages, as well as enough freshness to work with grilled sardines and salads. Spanish rosado is also delicious with these foods.

I especially like delicate and pretty rosés from Provence with the lightness-of-touch flavours inherent in Japanese food. Fruity rosés with depth of flavour and a hint of extra sugar, like those from the Loire, can go with subtly spicy dishes.

The versatility of rosé makes it a no-brainer picnic wine. While it's perky enough to work as an aperitif or with salads, the richer ones are great with charcuterie and goat's cheese, and the fruitier ones can also partner desserts. Try a Portuguese rosé.

Rosé is a catch-all option with most fish, but pink-fleshed fish and shellfish work especially well, whether it's salmon or prawns/shrimp, a dry rosé peps up these fishy flavours brilliantly. Try a dry Loire rosé or pink English fizz.

If sweet wine isn't your thing, then a punchy dry rosé can work well with dessert. If there are red fruits in the dessert, even better, because these have a natural affinity with the red-fruit flavours in the wines.

PICK THE RIGHT WINE: WHITE

Whether you know the grape you want, the flavour you are in the mood for, or the food you're eating, we all need a little shortcut at some point in our lives, so this is a quick reference guide for when it's that kind of moment.

Pinot Grigio → pear · elderflower

Albariño → floral · salty · zesty

Dry Muscat → grape

Dry (young) Riesling → lime · ginger

Verdejo → lemon · grapefruit

} fish
salads
spicy food
vegetables

delicate

Oaked Chardonnay → buttery · honey · mushroom

Oaked Chenin Blanc → waxy · creamy · mushroom

Oaked Viura (white Rioja) → smoky · vanilla · mushroom

} pork
poultry
mushroom

bold

medium-bodied

Sauvignon Blanc → herbaceous · passion fruit
Unoaked Chardonnay → melon · apple
Grüner Veltliner → herbaceous · citrus

} cheese
fish
salads
vegetables

Viognier → peach · apricot
Unoaked Chenin Blanc → nuts · grapefruit
Semillon → apple · nuts
Godello → peach
Gewürztraminer → rose petal · ginger
Pinot Gris → waxy · orange
Older Riesling → nuts · waxy
Torrontés → rose petal · citrus peel

} chicken
pork
poultry
spicy food

viognier *Say it: vee-on-ee-yay*

pungent

juicy

exotic

creamy

perfumed

luscious

A red grape masquerading as a white grape: that's how I once heard Viognier described. What a brilliant description! Viognier has attitude and oomph, and guts and texture, and it likes being blended into red wines. It's a red grape in all but colour.

I have a soft spot for Viognier because its flavour is very distinguishable. It's all about the peachy fruit, and when it's really good, beneath this luscious fruit there'll be extra layers of flavour: apricot, vanilla, honey and almond. Viognier isn't just used to make a fruity white wine either. It's also hugely important for pepping up the aroma and freshness in wines made from Syrah in the Rhône Valley in France. But that's not exclusive to France – you can find producers doing this in Australia, South Africa and the USA, too. Viognier is so pungent, you don't even need a large amount added into a red wine to make itself known; even the slightest of Viognier drops are noticeable when blended with Syrah/Shiraz. Viognier is also happy being blended with white grapes, and especially with other white grapes grown in the Rhône Valley, like Marsanne and Roussanne. Since around the millennium, Viognier has enjoyed a new lease of life, thanks to producers in Australia and California too, because before then, it only existed in very small quantities in France.

🏠 Rhône Valley, France

It's mind-blowing to think that before 2000, Viognier barely existed outside of this region. Here in its motherland, Viognier has two important roles. It can make a soft, peach-flavoured white wine and it's the grape behind one of the rarest white wines in the world – Condrieu. Its other role is to act as an aroma- and flavour-enhancer for red Syrah/Shiraz, especially in the Rhône sub-region of Côte-Rôtie.

Naming Viognier
Condrieu is one of the most expensive Viognier wines in the world. This is the name of a wine-producing region in the northern Rhône Valley, as well as the wine style made from the Viognier grape.

This grape...
SMELLS:
floral · spicy
TASTES OF:
apricot · dried fruit ·
honey · mango · peach
· pineapple · vanilla

> **Although Viognier is full-on in flavour, it's not known as a white wine that ages well because it's low in acid, which acts as a preservative for wines.**

viognier: **regions & flavours**

California

One of California's most successful white grapes, the juice factor in Viognier from California is off the charts. It's so intense, it's almost like sniffing, and drinking, a can of peaches in syrup. Cline Cellars in Sonoma produces some delicious full-flavoured examples with classic aromas of peach, apricot and honey.

Australia

In certain patches across Australia, Viognier has thrived in adversity, even though it's a pig of a variety to grow. This is because it takes a long time to ripen, but if it's too ripe it loses its freshness extremely quickly. Both on its own as a white wine (where the outcome is usually somewhere between the juiciness of California and the elegance of the Rhône) and as an addition to red wine, Viognier's worth is demonstrated by the fact that many of Australia's top Shiraz producers add a splash of it to their very best wines.

Yalumba is a producer that has gone to great pains to put Viognier back on the map here, and its Viognier is one of the best around. It comes from the southern Australian region Eden Valley, and is full-bodied, floral and silky-smooth.

South Africa

Maybe it's unfair to say that Viognier is hugely important to South Africa's white wine scene by default, because Syrah/Shiraz is also really important to South Africa, but the fact is, it is important because of this. Many a South African Syrah/Shiraz has Viognier in the mix, à la Rhône.

That said, there are some good white Viogniers to be had, too, especially when mixed into gorgeous white wine blends with Chenin Blanc (see pages 88–91), but also on their own. I especially like the varietal (single grape) style made by The Foundry in Stellenbosch.

Southern France

The Rhône Valley and the south of France often share grape varieties, so it's no surprise to learn that Viognier can be found in Languedoc-Roussillon, just not in vast quantities. These Viogniers are full of fleshy peach fruit but not as pungent as those from the New World. And what's more, they're often more affordable than those from the Rhône.

New Zealand

In the race to prove itself as more than a one-trick white wine pony (Sauvignon Blanc), other grapes in the catch-all group 'aromatics' include Viognier, which is proving to be pretty successful here, again albeit it in small volumes and both as a white wine and as a blend with some of its Syrah/Shiraz, which is especially good in the region of Hawke's Bay. I've tasted some lovely, fresh Viogniers from Marlborough, the land of Sauvignon Blanc, made by a producer called Churton.

chardonnay

concentrated
fresh
creamy
elegant
smoky
waxy
chewy

Call me an optimist, but I'm convinced there's a Chardonnay for everyone out there, even if it is one of those grapes that people seem to love or hate. Chardonnay's home is Burgundy, but because it's grown all over the world, and because it can be such a blank canvas, it's also pretty happy when blended with other grapes. Like it or loathe it, Chardonnay is one of the highest-quality wine grapes around.

It's one of the most popular grapes in the world, but because Chardonnay is naturally pretty neutral, it gets most of its flavour during the winemaking process, and there are two common ways to boost its flavour.

When you expose Chardonnay to oak, in barrels or by soaking the wine on wooden staves (planks), it soaks up the flavour like a sponge. This means that the winemaker has to be careful about the type of wood used when producing Chardonnay (see page 41). Chardonnay can go through the alcoholic fermentation in oak or it can be aged after fermentation. Winemakers who want lots of oaky flavour in their Chardonnay will do both.

For maximum richness in flavour – in addition to the oak – winemakers will let Chardonnay rest on its lees. Lees are the yeast deposits that are created after the wine goes through fermentation, so they add a yeasty flavour of bread and biscuits/cookies to the wine. Lees are also really important in contributing to the texture of Chardonnay in the mouth. More lees means more chewiness.

🏠 Burgundy, France

I'll happily confess it took me some time to get to grips with white Burgundy. All that buttery, toasty, nutty richness used to feel old-fashioned and heavy, but now I'm a total convert, so even if it doesn't work for you the first time around, I really recommend to keep giving it a try rather than shutting the door on it. Burgundian Chardonnay can have serious complexity and has a good ability to age. Chardonnay is *the* white wine grape of Burgundy and especially in the southern half of the main strip, the region called Côte de Beaune.

In descending order of prestige, white Burgundy (Chardonnay) is labelled:

🏆 Grand Cru
• Premier Cru
• (The name of a village), for example Meursault
• Bourgogne

This grape...

SMELLS:

appley • floral • grassy • herbaceous • nutty • oaky • smoky • toasty • waxy

TASTES OF:

apple • bacon • biscuit/cookie • brioche • butter • caramel • honey • lemon • melon • nuts • pastry • peach • pineapple • vanilla

chardonnay: regions & flavours

Chablis, France

There's much debate about whether this is part of Burgundy or not. Technically, it is in the same region, but if someone is referring to white Burgundy, that usually doesn't include Chablis. The reason it's so different in style is geographic as much as anything else. Chablis is much further north and cooler than the main stretch of Burgundy, so the wines usually have a fresher bite to them.

The term 'Chablis' refers to the general wine region, the town of Chablis itself, one of the hierarchies in the wine classification system *and* the name of the general wine style – it's no wonder people get confused. In descending order, the hierarchy categories run as follows: 'Grand Cru' then 'Premier Cru', followed by 'Chablis', then 'Petit Chablis'. Very generally speaking, the Chardonnays of these two highest classifications will usually have oak influence, while the lower two usually won't. And as for producers, some of my favourites include Moreau-Naudet and Vincent Dampt.

Champagne, France

I can't emphasize enough the importance of Chardonnay in Champagne. It's one of the region's three main grapes and is the only white one of those three. It gives Champagne a floral fragrance, and extra crispness in the mouth as well as the ability to age for a long time. When Champagne is made purely from Chardonnay it's called a 'Blanc de Blancs', roughly translated as 'white wine made from white grapes'. Some of my favourite Blanc de Blancs Champagnes come from the houses of Charles Heidsieck, Deutz, Delamotte and Larmandier-Bernier.

Spain

Chardonnay has become an important addition to the production of Cava, Spain's most famous sparkling wine. Whether it's blended with Pinot Noir, with native Spanish grapes, or used on its own, in recent years Chardonnay has really contributed to the improved quality of a lot of Cavas.

England

Stop press: Chardonnay is now hot stuff for English fizz (yes, of course I'm biased) in much the same way as it is important in Champagne. As this style of wine increases its international renown, so, too, does the amount of Chardonnay being planted, especially on England's south coast, which is thought to have a similar soil structure to Champagne. Who to try? Well, Coates & Seely in Hampshire and Nyetimber in West Sussex both make delicious Blanc de Blancs.

Franciacorta, Italy ★

Give Franciacorta a go. I say this with confidence, because if you like Champagne and Italian wine, I feel sure you won't be disappointed. Franciacorta is Italy's delicious answer to Champagne. And like Champagne, Franciacorta is the name of the region in Lombardy as well as the wine style made there. Chardonnay is the most popular grape used in Franciacorta. My tip is to look out for Satèn, a style of Franciacorta that has very silky-soft bubbles. It's fresh but also very food-friendly, and still (amazingly!) unknown outside of Italy. I really like the Franciacortas made by Fratelli Berlucchi, Monte Rossa and Bellavista. Still wines made from Chardonnay in the Franciacorta region have a different name, Curtefranca, and these can be delicious, too.

Australia

The infamous days of overblown butter bombs from Australia have mostly gone. Australia's done a great

job at toning down its Chardonnay in recent years, and although oak is still used, usually it's nowhere near as sickly or in-your-face as it used to be. Elegant Chardonnays can be found all over the country now, but one of my favourite regions is the Mornington Peninsula in Victoria, where Chardonnays can be super-refined. Here, I always enjoy Yabby Lake wines. But let's not forget western Australia, either, where Leeuwin Estate and Vasse Felix are names to look out for. In Tasmania, it's cool enough to make fresh and zingy sparkling wine from Chardonnay. Jansz makes some lovely sparkling wine there.

New Zealand

Chardonnay is a buzzword in New Zealand right now. The climate's freshness makes deliciously clear and crisp Chardonnay, often with good melon and apple fruit flavours, and I always find it to be brilliantly versatile with food. One of the best things about Chardonnay made here is the consistency, some regions have more experience than others in making this grape but all the regions seem to be excited about the potential of Chardonnay, and I'm just as enthusiastic as they are. Of the NZ Chardonnays I've tasted, I've really enjoyed those from Ngatarawa (Alwyn), Kumeu River and Giesen.

USA

The quality of Chardonnay in the US can vary hugely, ranging from beguilingly beautiful to, if I'm being perfectly honest, downright boring and tasteless. So, what to do? Well, the painful truth is that price is often a good guide, so if in doubt, spend as much as you can afford – it's usually worth it. If you like your Chardonnay smoky, toasty and with rich, bacon-fat flavours, the USA is the place for you. Napa really champions Californian Chardonnay, and charges prices to match – two of my favourite producers are Mi Sueno and Truchard. But if you look further north, in the Russian River Valley, you can find great unoaked Chardonnays from places like Marimar Estate. Watch out for the freshness of Chardonnays coming out of Washington State – they have a buttery richness but a salty tang to boot. I really enjoy those from Januik and Woodward Canyon.

Organic, biodynamic, natural

What's an organic wine?
Organic wine today means that everything from grape- growing to bottling the final wine is done organically, which includes rules such as the banning of synthetic chemical fertilizers, pesticides and herbicides in the vineyard, and capping the amount of sulphur that's used as a preservative. After three years of proven organic practice, wine producers can apply for organic certification from official bodies such as ECOCERT. The term 'organic wine' only came into being in 2012. Before that, wines could only be described as being made 'from organically grown grapes'.

Where do organic wines come from?
Grapes with the best chance of organic success are in warm and dry climates because there's less chance of disease, and therefore fewer chemical treatments are needed for the grapes to survive.

Can a wine be organic and not certified?
Yes. Many producers adhere to organic wine practices without seeking accreditation from an official body.

What's the difference between biodynamic and organic?
People often confuse the two, because the French word for organic wine is the widely used term 'bio' (short for *biologique*), while biodynamic is *biodynamie*! Anyway, being biodynamic is totally different to being organic because it's more spiritual, that's to say the people who follow it have a belief in a philosophy rather than think of it as a practice to be followed. Biodynamic producers make their wines with respect to the environment so the whole production system is healthy and harmonious for the environment. Most famously, this includes respecting the different influences of the cosmos on growing conditions. For example, the position of the moon and the stars has a bearing on when and if certain procedures happen; so do the time of the year and the time of the day. Producers with a proven biodynamic record can also get certification – one official certifier is DEMETER.

What's a natural wine?
Natural wine has captured the zeitgeist of the 2010s because of a belief (by some, who are still in a minority) that the modern wine world has become increasingly homogenized. The people who make natural wines believe wine is 'cleaned up' so much in the production process that wines around the world have become indistinguishable.
There's no set definition of a natural wine, though, and everyone has their own opinion on what it should be. It's a holistic approach, so the levels of 'naturalness' can vary from producer to producer. Essentially, though, it means a wine that's made with as little interference as possible – this includes using natural yeasts and organically grown grapes. Sulphur is one of the key issues in the natural wine debate, because without sulphur, wines generally have a shorter shelf life; they oxidize more quickly, changing their colour, and sometimes leading to a vinegary aroma.

What are Fairtrade® wines?
The Fairtrade® initiative involves local sustainability and the production of products made by people in the developing world who are provided with decent working conditions, all in an effort to improve their quality of life. It also includes fair terms of trade, so prices must never fall lower than the market price.

sauvignon blanc

tangy
fresh
herbal
sour
juicy
vibrant
zesty

France is the home of Sauvignon Blanc, but New Zealand is where its style trends begin. When New Zealand sprang onto the wine scene back in the 1980s, its Sauvignon Blanc was hard to ignore thanks to its insanely tropical fruit flavours.

Today, New Zealand Sauvignon Blanc has become so universally loved that even the more traditional Sauvignon Blanc regions are making wines in a copycat style. And now, just to keep the trends coming, New Zealand has started making sparkling Sauvignon Blanc.

Sauvignon Blanc isn't fussy about where it grows and it's always packed with flavour, making it a hugely popular wine grape wherever it's made. Plus it can be made into anything: dry or sweet, still or sparkling.

🏠 Loire Valley, France

This valley in northern France is home to those famous Sauvignon Blanc-growing villages of Pouilly-Fumé and Sancerre, which, as you might recognize, also give their names to the wine style. These wines are known for being delicate and zesty, with herbaceous flavours and minerality. They're a hugely popular choice on wine lists, because they have such a good reputation, and although they're exquisite, they can sometimes be overpriced. If you want a decent Loire Sauvignon without the price tag of the famous villages, try Sauvignon de Touraine, which is also from the same valley and can be great value for money.

Did you know?
Sauvignon Blanc falls under the umbrella term 'aromatics' for pungent grapes, and is a parent to the red grape Cabernet Sauvignon (see pages 36–40). It also loves to be blended with Semillon, especially in the production of sweet wines (see pages 92–95 and 122–125).

This grape...

SMELLS:
floral · grassy ·
herbaceous · perfumed
· zesty

TASTES OF:
asparagus ·
elderflower ·
grapefruit · lemon ·
lime · mango · nettle ·
passion fruit · pea ·
peach · pear

sauvignon blanc: regions & flavours

Bordeaux, France

Sauvignon Blanc has two jobs in Bordeaux. Firstly, it's used to make a light, dry wine. Sometimes it is used on its own to do this, but it's more common to find it blended with Semillon. These dry whites are usually crisp, citrus-fresh and herbaceous, similar to the ones in the Loire Valley, but generally a bit chewier in the mouth. Secondly, it is used to make sweet wines. Again, these are usually blended with Semillon, and sometimes with another white grape called Muscadelle. The wines are honeyed, with a delicious marmalade and candied orange flavour. Famous regions (and again, style names) are Sauternes and Barsac.

New Zealand

This is where the new generation of Sauvignon Blanc began, and these wines reek of tropical fruits like passion fruit, mango and pineapple; sometimes, they even smell of sweat. Marlborough is the South Island region where this country's Sauvignon Blanc hype began, and largely thanks to one producer, Cloudy Bay.

Today, Sauvignon Blanc is a signature wine for all of the country's winemaking regions, although Marlborough is still thought of as the epicentre. There are almost too many good producers to choose from, but among my favourites outside of Marlborough are Craggy Range and Neudorf. In Marlborough itself, I'm a fan of Seresin, Jackson Estate, Isabel Estate and Dog Point. Cloudy Bay is famous for putting NZ wine on the map, but it also makes a gorgeous oaky version of 'straight' Sauvignon Blanc called Te Koko, and this is the style that is becoming more popular to make here.

USA

America has made a serious contribution to the Sauvignon Blanc world stage – putting it in contact with oak barrels (see page 41). This style usually goes by the name of Fumé Blanc and is most often found in the USA. However, and although it's still pretty niche, it's a growing trend around the world.

I don't mind admitting it took me some time to get my head around this style of wine. I mean, when a grape naturally has so much character, as Sauvignon Blanc does, why try to smother it with the flavour of oak? Well, the answer is that the best ones are not slathered in oaky flavour, instead, the oak is used to build up the body and texture of the Sauvignon Blanc.

This style dumbs down the vibrancy of flavours in Sauvignon Blanc. They often have a smoky, earthy character as the wood deliberately calms down the full-on fruitiness of the wine, but also makes the wine incredibly food-friendly. Some of the best producers of this style include Robert Mondavi and Ferrari-Carano, both in California.

Italy

'Italy?' I hear you ask. Yes, Italy. It's only made in small proportions over in the north-eastern region of Friuli, but they make some delicious, citrus, grapefruit-flavoured, sour, dry wines using Sauvignon Blanc. They're underrated, so if you have a chance, try one. Give Visintini a whirl – it makes a delicious Sauvignon Blanc.

Trends

These days, some Loire producers are trying to emulate the New Zealand Sauvignon by making more tropical-flavoured wines and putting Kiwi-related images and wording on the label.

 One of the most recent Sauvignon Blanc trends is to make it in oak barrels, which dumbs down the aroma, but is thought to make a wine that is more likely to age well

Chile

Improving in quality all the time, Chile can make fantastic Sauvignon Blanc. When looking for the best that Chile has to offer, look out for regions that are close to the sea, like Casablanca, which is the traditional white wine Mecca for top-quality Chilean white wines. One of the most exciting things about the Chilean wine scene at the moment is the new regions, like Limari Valley and a tiny little area called Paradones. Both of these regions make juicy Sauvignon Blancs, but with a zesty grapefruit freshness and a salty tang, because their vineyards are surrounded by sea air. There are loads of great examples, but some of my favourites are Casa Silva Cool Coast and Undurraga Terroir Hunter.

South Africa

They might not thank me for this, but South African Sauvignon Blanc grapes make wines that are often described as halfway between the delicate Sauvignon from the Loire Valley and the tropical fruitiness of the southern hemisphere. Based on the wines I have tasted, I think that's a fair description. My favourite region? Elgin. And here, the producer Iona makes some very cool wines. That said, Durbanville is another region making crisp and cool South African Sauvignon Blanc.

Australia

Sauvignon Blanc is made all over Australia, but it's best known when it's blended with Semillon (see pages 92–95). The region it's made in is crucial, because Sauvignon Blanc thrives in cooler spots. This means regions like Adelaide Hills in South Australia have the advantage over the country's hot spots.

Making sweet wines

Sweet wines like Sauternes rely on the grapes being infected by a 'good' disease called Botrytis cinerea or 'noble rot'. This disease pierces the skins of the berries, causing the water inside to evaporate, leaving behind a berry with a high sugar concentration from which the wine is then made.

Party wines

It doesn't matter how much you like it, a party is no time to crack open a quirky, off-beat wine. The most successful party wines are well known and classic, because it's much better to have people actually drink the wine than be left with cases of the stuff afterwards. So yes, crowd-pleasing, well-known classics are the way to go, and the ones that usually work best are the ones that shout 'LOOK AT ME!' when they're in the glass and in the mouth. You want obvious wines, not wimpy wines, and if possible, ones that are going to match a range of food, too. If I had a choice of five wine styles to pour at a party, it would be these.

Should I serve fizz?

Some people demand it, some people expect it, and even if they weren't expecting it and are greeted with a glass, everyone at a party loves fizz. Champagne is the ultimate in luxury, so if the budget stretches that far, it's a crowd-pleasing no-brainer. Although Prosecco is easier on the party budget, it can get drowned out in the roar of a party, so I often go for a Crémant instead, which is French – so many people will assume it's a Champagne anyway (they'll think you've been very generous!). It's made in the same way as Champagne, so it has class, but usually comes in at half the price.

Which white?

Sauvignon Blanc is one of the most identifiable wine flavours in the world. It can smell and taste of anything from freshly mown grass to green vegetables and from citrus to exotic fruit. But the point here is that its flavour is loved by many, known by many and it can match many foods. Plus, a decent one doesn't cost the earth.

Which rosé?

A dry rosé is a great party wine. It's very versatile with food and it looks attractive, especially if you have a deeply coloured one, which is easy enough to find if you buy one from the New World, Spain or Portugal, or if it's made from Syrah/Shiraz or Cabernet Sauvignon.

Which red?

BEAUJOLAIS Bursting with juicy red fruits and full of life, a young and bouncy Beaujolais is great with all sorts of food. If you want the richest type of Beaujolais to match, say, red meat, or you have a decent budget, get a Cru, like Morgon; if you want something cheaper, the next step down – but still a delicious and friendly version – would say 'Beaujolais-Villages' on the label.
SYRAH/SHIRAZ It's hard to beat a robust red like Syrah/Shiraz. Not only do you get decent bang for your buck, it packs in plenty of flavour, and in summer, it's the perfect match for a barbecue.

Are there other ways to serve wine?

PINK PORT CRUSH (SUMMER COCKTAIL) Pink Port makes a brilliant base for a summery, fresh cocktail. Use it as a base, then top it up with elderflower cordial and tonic water, with loads of ice and quartered strawberries to garnish. It's the ultimate refreshing summer drink.
MULLED PALO CORTADO (WINTER COCKTAIL) My take on the standard mulled wine is a gorgeous winter-warming alternative. Pour a bottle of dry palo cortado into a saucepan or pot set over a gentle heat. Add 40 ml/1½ oz. of ginger liqueur, 4 dried figs, 3 whole cloves, 4 teaspoons of clear honey, the grated zest of 1 orange, 1 cinnamon stick and 1 whole nutmeg, grated. Warm until hot, without boiling, then strain and serve.

chenin blanc

fresh

dry

waxy

rich

creamy

chewy

sweet

If you're new to wine, chances are Chenin Blanc isn't going to blow your mind. I say this because often when I show Chenin Blanc to people I often get this 'so what?' look in return. But persevere with it, please, because this is a classic case of not judging a book by its cover.

You see, Chenin Blanc is a complex grape and can make a complex wine. It's a bit like Chardonnay on the face of things, in the sense that it's relatively neutral. It hasn't got the wham-bam-thank-you-ma'am aroma satisfaction of, say, a Sauvignon Blanc; instead it's quiet and reserved, and takes time to open out.

Chenin Blanc is made into all styles of wine: still and sparkling, dry, off-dry and full-on sweet wines, although most of its flavour typically comes from one or a combination of three things – age, oak and lees. Older vintages of good Chenin Blanc can be gorgeous, and it has the capacity to age for a long time too – I'm talking decades, so seek out older styles if you can. As with Chardonnay, when Chenin Blanc has spent time in contact with oak, it takes on a nutty flavour and chewy texture. Usually, this will boost its food-friendly credentials. Lees are the yeast deposits left after fermentation, and it's very common practice to let a Chenin Blanc 'sit' on the lees after the wine has been made. When this happens, the wine soaks up more yeasty flavour and, just like with the oak, can give an extra chewiness and richness to the wine.

So how does it taste? Well, Chenin Blanc can be chirpy and zesty in the first flush of youth, nutty and waxy if it's a bit older or has some oak on it, or can be a gorgeous, sticky, unctuous mouthful of marmalade and orange when it's sweet.

Want to know about oak's influence on a wine's flavour? See page 41.

Want to know about fizz made from Chenin Blanc? See pages 128–129.

🏠 Loire Valley, France

If this were a book with sound effects, this chapter would sound like a long, deep and satisfied sigh because Chenin Blanc can make some truly hedonistic white wines from here, whether dry or sweet. Wines that are from the Loire villages of Vouvray, Quarts de Chaume, Bonnezeaux and Montlouis make delicious sweet versions of Chenin Blanc. The grapes for these wines are picked late off the vine, which means they have a high concentration of sugar. For medium-sweet Chenin Blanc, the region of Vouvray is perhaps the most famous village (and style) – it's deliciously fruity, and not sickly at all, while Savennières is the region that really champions bone-dry Chenin Blanc. Some of my favourite Chenin Blanc producers in the Loire include Domaine Huet and Nicolas Joly.

This grape...

SMELLS:

floral · herbaceous · oaky

TASTES OF:

apple · apricot · biscuit/cookie · butter · honey · lemon · melon · mushroom · nuts · peach · pear

chenin blanc: regions & flavours

South Africa

Chenin Blanc is South Africa's flagship white grape and there's twice as much Chenin Blanc planted here as there is in the Loire, which only goes to show just how seriously this country takes this grape. Like in France, it's used for everything from dry to sweet and rocks up all over the country. One of the reasons it does well here is that there's a good supply of old Chenin Blanc vines, which are said to add complexity in the grapes and, subsequently, the wine. These wines can be complex, nutty and full of honeyed flavours. The best ones carry all of these things, but are zingy and fresh, too.

One of the most exciting white wine developments for me in the last few years happened in Cape Town, in 2012. You might call it an epiphany, and it began when I tasted a beautiful white blend called Cartology, made by Chris Alheit. It tasted of lemon peel and ripe apple, but it was also savoury and earthy. This wine was just the beginning of an adventure of gorgeous white blends I tasted during that trip, and I've been an avid fan ever since.

These white blended wines are often based on Chenin Blanc, with smaller amounts of other grapes added in, sometimes made up of five or six grapes, sometimes a lot more; and I think we're at the beginning of seeing this trend develop further, or at least I hope we are.

Some of my favourite Chenin Blanc producers, whether it's straight Chenins or blends include Chris Alheit, Sequillo, Mullineux, Sadie Family, Adi Badenhorst and Ken Forrester.

USA

There are smatterings of Chenin Blanc to be found across the USA. In California though, especially in the Central Valley, Chenin Blanc has a bit of a tainted reputation because massive yields of the grape leave it with little flavour, and so a lot of this kind of Chenin Blanc is blended away with a white grape (that isn't particularly illustrious) called Colombard. Made this way, you can see why people don't get very excited about it. But that's not to say there aren't a few highlights in this state, the region of Clarksburg in the Sacramento Delta is doing a decent job at showing Chenin Blanc's true potential, while in Sonoma, try the Chenin Blanc from Dry Creek Vineyard. Meanwhile on the east coast, Paumanok Vineyards on Long Island is known for its cult Chenin Blanc following.

New Zealand

Chenin Blanc is super-niche here, and is in fact mostly championed by one producer! In the North Island region of Gisborne, Millton Vineyard farms biodynamically and does such a good job with Chenin Blanc that more than half of the wine they make comes from this grape. Its dry Chenin Blanc tastes both citrus fresh with a little honey richness and shows the true class we know this grape can achieve.

Look out for Chenin Blanc 👁

Chenin Blanc has synonyms – it's sometimes called 'Anjou' in the Loire Valley or 'Steen' in South Africa, which is the Dutch word for 'stone'. Whatever it's called, Chenin Blanc is the darling of the funky new white blends coming out of South Africa, especially from the region of Swartland.

semillon *Say it: sem-ee-yon (in Australia they pronounce the 'll's, everywhere else they're silent)*

fresh

dry

succulent

creamy

waxy

sweet

luscious

Semillon is one of those grapes that does more than most people realize. In Bordeaux, its influence is massive, because not only is it a crucial blending partner with Sauvignon Blanc to make dry white wines, but it's also one of the key grapes in the sexy sweet wines of Sauternes and Barsac.

Why do they work so well together? Because Semillon and Sauvignon Blanc have a yin-yang relationship. Sauvignon Blanc can seem austere and uptight to some people, but when you throw the fatter, oilier Semillon into the mix, the tension in Sauvignon Blanc relaxes; you can almost hear it breathe a sigh of relief. Ultimately, this combination makes a fruity and well-rounded wine.

Semillon doesn't always need Sauvignon Blanc, though. It works on its own, too, although it doesn't have masses of natural flavour. When it's made for very early drinking it can be grassy and zesty, and when it's ripe, it will be full and round. Some of the most delectable dry Semillons I've ever tasted have come from Australia once they've been aged a good seven or eight years – this is when they taste of almonds and baked apples, and have a deep golden colour. Semillon is found all over the world these days, but the places that champion it most are Bordeaux and Australia.

🏠 Bordeaux, France

As I mentioned above, the relationship between Sauvignon Blanc and Semillon works a dream here in Bordeaux, where they're made into dry, light wines that are made to be drunk when the wines are young, nippy and zesty. In Sauternes and Barsac, Semillon is a crucial component in making the honeyed, candied fruit and unctuous sweet wines of these regions (and wine styles with the same name). When Semillon is crafted into this style of wine, it can age for much longer than a dry version of the wine would.

Did you know?
Dry white Bordeaux wines are usually a blend of Sauvignon Blanc and Semillon.

This grape…

SMELLS:

**grassy · herbaceous ·
tropical · zesty**

TASTES OF:

**apple · dried fruit ·
grapefruit · honey ·
lemon · lime · nuts**

semillon: regions & flavours

Australia

Australia has really taken Semillon under its wing, so much so you could almost say it's the flagship white grape. A region in New South Wales called Hunter Valley (sometimes just shortened to 'Hunter') makes gorgeous wines from pure Semillon.

The vines here are very old, too, and, like with Chenin Blanc in South Africa, older vines are thought to add increased complexity to the wine. Hunter Semillons that are eight to 10 years old have a gorgeous waxy, biscuity/cookie character, while they're smooth and supple on the palate. They are real wines to savour. Tyrrell's Vat 1 Hunter Semillon is always sold a little bit older than other white wines and is a classic of this great Australian style.

Hunter Valley isn't the only place to find lush Australian Semillon, though. It's also made into a polished white wine in the Clare Valley and Margaret River area in Western Australia.

Meet Muscadelle

One of Semillon's most important roles in the world of wine is as a sweet wine, but Muscadelle is a French grape that often pops up in the same places as Semillon. Its best contribution is to making sweet wines, partly because Muscadelle has very thin skin. When a grape has a thin skin, it's more susceptible to disease, and one of the 'good' grape diseases, Botrytis cinerea, is responsible for making some of the most mind-blowing sweet wines in the world (see page 86), so step forward Muscadelle. Yes, Muscadelle is sometimes used with Sauvignon Blanc and Semillon to make those sticky Bordeaux wines of Sauternes and Barsac. However, it's more used – and more famous in a region not too far from Bordeaux, Bergerac, for one sweet wine in particular: the gorgeous marmalade-flavoured Monbazillac. Muscadelle also crops up in Australia, which, as we know, is important for Semillon too. Like in France, it makes both dry and sweet wines but the best ones by far are those sweet wines made in Rutherglen, Victoria, in Australia. Here, producers often call it 'Rutherglen Topaque'. Topaque used to be known as 'Tokay', because they thought the grape originally came from Tokaj in Hungary. Give the Rutherglen Topaques from Stanton & Killeen or Campbells a go.

muscat

perfumed
dry
light
exotic
fresh
sweet
luscious

Muscat is a grape which, for once, actually smells and tastes like a grape. It often confuses people, though, because its name changes frequently, depending on the country of origin (Moscatel in Spain and Portugal, Moscato in Italy, Moschato in Greece) and because it can be, and is, made into a still or sparkling, dry or sweet, and a table or fortified wine. Because of this, I look at this grape according to style rather than region, just to make things really clear.

Muscat is also a grape that mutates very easily, so there are tonnes of variations of it, so this section is dedicated to the highest-quality one, Muscat Blanc à Petits Grains. Although it doesn't make a dry, light wine very often, it's a useful little grape for pepping up the aroma and flavour in wines that are more neutral.

Muscat Blanc à Petits Grains grows all across France in different varieties from different regions that are included in the names of the grapes – Muscat de Frontignan, Muscat d'Alsace, Muscat de Beaumes-de-Venise – as well as all over Piedmont in Italy. Other Muscat classifications include Muscat Ottonel and Muscat d'Alexandrie, which are slightly inferior to the Muscat Blanc à Petits Grains I look at here. Muscat is an ancient grape variety and because it's so old there's constant discussion over where its true 'home' lies. For Muscat Blanc à Petits Grains, many people believe the answer is Greece, from where it's thought to have spread across Europe. Over the years this grape has mutated so much, its possible to find versions of this grape that are pink and black as well as its best known colour, white.

Gewürztraminer *Say it: guh-vertztra-meener*

Muscat and Gewürztraminer are both famous for having an incredibly strong perfume. Found across northern Europe, Gewürz (as it's often called) is increasingly turning up in New World countries such as New Zealand, Australia and Chile. It makes both a dry and sweet wine, and is found by itself as well as blended with other grapes. Its typical characters are rose, lychee and ginger so it's commonly used to pep up the aroma of a more subtle grape. Gewürz is happiest when grown in cooler climates, both to preserve this special perfume and because it's a grape that can reach high levels of sugar (and therefore alcohol).

This grape...
SMELLS:
floral • perfumed
TASTES OF:
apple • apricot • grape
• ginger • lemon •
orange • pear •
sultana/golden raisin

 Vin doux naturel is a fortified sweet wine whose alcohol fermentation is stopped deliberately early; this means it has a high level of sugar, leaving the wine sweet.

muscat: regions & flavours

Dry or slightly sweet
ALSACE, FRANCE
Muscat is one of the key white grapes grown in Alsace and makes cute, light wines. They are delicate, classically grapey in flavour and pair well with Asian dishes, especially when lemongrass is the main ingredient. Charles Schléret and Hugel both make delicious dry Muscats. Alsace makes sweet wines, too, of course, but these are not generally made from Muscat. The sweeter ones will say Vendange Tardive (VT) or Sélection de Grains Nobles (SGN) on the label.

Slightly sweet & sparkling
ITALY
Moscato is usually found in the north of Italy – it's the most planted white grape in Piedmont because it's used to make Asti and the superior Moscato d'Asti.

Moscato d'Asti ★
This is a moreish, delicate and underrated wine – it's my go-to wine as a lighter style of dessert wine. It isn't as sparkling or as high in alcohol as Asti. Moscato d'Asti has a pretty elderflower taste, which, combined with its gentle spritz and low alcohol (usually around 5% ABV – alcohol by volume), makes it a great wine to finish off a meal with, because you have a little hit of sweetness without any of the richness that can come from typical sweet wines. Vajra, Elio Perrone and Poderi Einaudi all make delicious Moscato d'Astis.

RHÔNE VALLEY, FRANCE
Clairette de Die is a neat little sparkling wine that's mostly made from Muscat (a minimum of 75%). It's another pretty, lightly fizzy wine that tastes of honey and honeysuckle, and has around 7% ABV.

Sweet
ROUSSILLON, FRANCE
Muscat de Rivesaltes is the name given to a *vin doux naturel* (fortified sweet wine) made here in the south of France. These are full-on sweet wines and can carry higher alcohol levels too (sometimes 16–17% ABV). When young, they taste of apricots and tropical fruits, and when older, they take on a nutty, orange flavour. This style is made with a proportion of Muscat Blanc à Petits Grains together with Muscat d'Alexandrie.

Sweet & fortified
AUSTRALIA
Liqueur Muscat is a gorgeous and ancient-tasting fortified wine made in the state of Victoria – the area of Rutherglen considers it a speciality, and often it's referred to as Rutherglen Muscat. These Muscats are sweet and complex, and are aged for long periods in wood, where they become incredibly intense wines that smell of tobacco and wood, and taste of caramel and treacle/molasses.

GREECE
Most sweet Greek Moschatos are *vin doux naturels*. Sweet Greek Moschatos are usually a dark-orange or amber colour, and many of the Greek islands make a version of this wine, although those made on the island of Samos are especially famous and good. The local cooperative in Samos makes most of the wines on the island. They taste of toffee, nuts and marmalade, and are deliciously unctuous. The flavours last a long time on the palate and they're delicious with a slice of orange cake.

riesling
Say it: reeze-ling (it's Riesling like breeze-ling, not rise-ling)

dry

perfumed

vibrant

fresh

exotic

elegant

delicate

sweet

luscious

Don't turn the page! Look, I know Riesling can be a massive no-no for some people, but one of the sad truths about this delicious grape is that when people don't realize they're drinking Riesling they actually love it. And so they should, because Riesling makes some of the classiest white wines in the world, and for this reason it's really respected by those in-the-know.

Despite this, it still suffers from two major misconceptions: people think it's low-quality or sweet. Some people think it's both, so let's take a closer look at these accusations.

'Riesling is low-quality.' This stems from the days of Liebfraumilch, that cheap, sugar-water German wine that had its heyday in the 1960s and '70s. The truth? Liebfraumilch wasn't even Riesling most of the time! But yes, Riesling is Germany's signature grape and it makes some of the purest, most complex white wines in the world.

'All Riesling is sweet.' So much Riesling is dry. Like, bone-dry. Yes, it can be hard to determine what is and isn't sweet sometimes, and if more wine bottles adopted the international sweetness scale on the back of their labels, our lives, and Riesling's life, would be much easier. Yes, there are sweet Rieslings, but what's wrong with that anyway? They can be some of the most remarkable wines in the world.

Still unconvinced? Then just try Riesling with food. It's an incredible food-pairing wine, especially with Asian dishes (see pages 156–161) plus it's often low in alcohol. And finally, it's super-fruity, which is why so many people love it when they taste it anonymously. Riesling is also great at retaining its identity from place to place, so it can be more difficult to distinguish one region from another than with other grapes.

🏠 Germany

German Riesling can taste like one of the purest wines in the world. The best can age really well, because their high acidity, and therefore freshness, gives them the ability to age. When this happens they can turn from wines packed with elderflower and floral aromas, full of lemon and lime flavours when young, to having a rich, honeyed and kerosene flavour. One of the most famous regions is Mosel, and Rieslings from here are pretty, delicate and have an elderflower purity with zingy freshness. This region has such a cool climate that the slightly sweeter style of Riesling works really well at softening the crisp acidity.

Want to know the sweetness levels on German Riesling? Look for the international Riesling scale on the back of bottles.

This grape...

SMELLS:
floral · herbaceous ·
perfumed · of petrol/
gasoline

TASTES OF:
elderflower · green
apple · honey · lemon ·
lime · passion fruit ·
peach · pineapple ·
orange

riesling: **regions & flavours**

Alsace, France

Alsace is the main French region for Riesling and the go-to place for dry, food-friendly wines, because Alsace Riesling is often dry and when it's super-sweet you'll find the words 'Vendange Tardive' (VT) or 'Sélections de Grains Nobles' (SGN) on the label. Grand Cru wines have come from the best vineyards.

Generally, Rieslings from Alsace don't have the full-on, pungent aroma that you find in Germany, but they are still very serious wines, and seriously elegant too. Some of my favourite producers are Trimbach, Hugel, Domaine Weinbach, Bott-Geyl and Albert Mann.

Austria

In Austria, Riesling plays second fiddle to native grape Grüner Veltliner, but it shouldn't be ignored as it cuts a really nice halfway house between the fruitiness of German Riesling and the texture and weight in the mouth of those you get in Alsace. Austria's most famous region is Wachau, where hot days and cool nights help to make the Riesling grapes smell especially fragrant. The Wachau Rieslings from Weingut Knoll and Weingut Prager are gorgeous.

USA

Both the East Coast and West Coast of North America are going gangbusters for Riesling. The Washington State sub-region, Columbia Valley, feels like the spiritual home of Riesling in the USA – it's also home to the world's largest Riesling producer, Chateau Ste Michelle. This estate, together with German Riesling supremo Ernie Loosen, makes a delicious Riesling from here, called Eroica. Another couple of great Riesling producers here are Charles Smith and Efeste¯.

On the East Coast, it's the Finger Lakes in New York that's making waves with Riesling right now. The harsh conditions here can be painfully cold, but it

means hardy Riesling thrives in most years, although some years it can even be too cold for Riesling. These often dry wines are not as aromatic as others, but they are more generous than European Rieslings in the mouth. Think of them as European Riesling without ice cubes – these are rounder and fruitier. Dr Konstantin Frank makes some lovely wines here; so, too, does Hermann J. Wiemer.

Australia

Australian Riesling is the most distinctive Riesling in my mind, because of their strong lime character. They are über-crisp, clear and pure, but also have an exotic twist. The best regions are in South Australia; Clare Valley and Eden Valley. Cool winds at night keep the Riesling from becoming too big and blowsy. Grosset, Pewsey Vale and Clos Clare make some gorgeous versions of zesty, floral, dry Riesling.

New Zealand

There are Riesling highlights throughout the country, but my go-to regions are all in the South Island. The most famous is the Waipara Valley, and Riesling here ranges from being German in style, with pure fruit, to Alsace in style, when it is more minerally. But be warned: the sweetness levels here can vary, although they're pretty good at declaring the sweetness on the label. Spy Valley and Pegasus Bay wines are lovely. Then there's Marlborough, check out Te Whare Ra's Riesling – delicious. It's also the main white grape in Central Otago, which has plenty of vineyards on schist soils, perfect for Riesling. Peregrine and Prophet's Rock make zingy, dry Rieslings here.

" When people don't realize they're tasting Riesling, they usually love it because it's so fruity, plus it's often a brilliant partner with Asian dishes. "

pinot grigio/pinot gris

perfumed
fresh
chewy
light
subtle

It's hard to be honest about Pinot Grigio without sounding like a complete snob, but the truth is that Pinot Grigio is a lot more famous for being fashionable than for being a complex wine. But maybe that's part of its appeal, a friend once told me she liked Pinot Grigio because it tasted of nothing!

I totally understand why people get confused between Pinot Grigio and its alter ego, Pinot Gris. I mean, it is the same grape, but there's usually a world of difference in the taste and complexity, because when wines are labelled Pinot Gris, they generally have a deeper, richer flavour. New World producers will produce both Pinot Grigio and Pinot Gris, each with its own distinct style according to the name.

But back to Pinot Grigio for a moment. It's a grape that has taken the world by storm in the last decade or so. It makes a light, crisp white that tastes of pear drops/hard candy, and because its popularity has gone ballistic, every winemaking country is cashing in on it, from Australia to Argentina.

🏠 France

Pinot Gris, we *think*, started out in Burgundy, because it's actually a version of Pinot Noir that became white over the years. But not many people today think of it that way, now that Pinot Grigio – its Italian incarnation – is so ubiquitous. So today, it's rare to find Pinot Gris in Burgundy, where it's sometimes called 'Pinot Beurot', but thanks to an ancient law, it's still permissible to use a tiny drop of Pinot Gris in red Burgundy, although I can't imagine this ever happens these days. The most famous French region for Pinot Gris is the north-eastern region of Alsace, where it makes both a sweet and dry wine, and generally has more guts and depth to it than the Italian Pinot Grigio.

The Aromatics Family
Pinot Grigio is one of the white grapes that falls under the 'aromatics' umbrella, together with Sauvignon Blanc, Riesling and Gewürztraminer.

This grape...

SMELLS:

floral · grassy · herbaceous · pear · perfumed

TASTES OF:

apple · apricot · citrus · grapefruit · lemon · nuts · pear · pear drops/candy

"If you want an Italian Pinot Grigio with attitude, try one from Friuli – you might have to pay a little bit more but it's worth it.

pinot grigio/pinot gris:
regions & flavours

Veneto, Italy

This north-eastern region is home to the masses of Pinot Grigio that set the trend around the world. It's for early drinking, should be drunk very cold, and tastes of pear drops/hard candy, and grapefruit, too, if you're lucky. Its popularity has one advantage, though: it's made us sit up and take notice of Italian white wines in general (see page 108), even if Pinot Grigio is still by far the most popular. Take a look at those from Pasqua, Masi and È Solo.

Friuli, Italy

Of all the Pinot Grigio versions that now exist, my favourites hail from this little pocket of north-eastern Italy, where super-crisp white wines are made in general. Here, Pinot Grigio tends to have more concentration than that from the Veneto. The best ones I've tried have a really strong, lemon-peel concentration to the fruit flavours, even if they are still frisky, early-drinking wines. Try the dry, full-bodied Grigios with their rich, floral and fruity aroma from Visintini and Jermann.

Alsace, France ★

It's incredible to think how delicious Alsace Pinot Gris can be, as opposed to the lighter Pinot Grigios from around the world. Alsace makes textbook Pinot Gris with flavours of apples and nuts, and it can even taste round and buttery. Plus, it can age well. It's brilliantly food-friendly and subtle in style, but has many layers of flavour. Usually, it comes in one of those tall, flute-shaped bottles but don't let that put you off (if you think these are for sweeter wines) – it's often dry in style. There's a bank of producers here that make excellent Pinot Gris, and I really rate

Josmeyer, Hugel and Domaine Weinbach.

USA

Oregon and Washington State make Pinot Gris; that's to say they are more Alsace in style, with a chewy texture and a nutty flavour to add to the fruit. California hasn't missed a trick, either, with this über-popular grape, and it makes both Grigio and Gris. Try those from Ponzi or Rex Hill.

New Zealand

Depending on the producer's whim, the styles here are either Grigio or Gris. But hopes are high in New Zealand that they can capitalize on people's love of the Pinot Grigio grape, especially because this country is so good at making the other 'aromatic' grapes, including its top dog, Sauvignon Blanc. Try the Grigio from Seifried or the Gris from Isabel Estate, Prophet's Rock or Eradus.

Grigio versus Gris

Grigio is usually reserved for wines that are pretty with sweet, floral aromas and are drunk very young. Gris is a richer-tasting version of the grape, with more waxy flavours, and is sometimes buttery, too. They are good with Asian food and can usually be enjoyed at an older age than most Grigio.

italian whites

Pinot Grigio set the world alight at the beginning of 21st century with its light and fruity style, opening the door for other Italian whites to follow. And, boy, did they follow! These are just a few of the very tasty Italian whites to look out for.

Falanghina
CENTRAL ITALY

A dry, nutty-flavoured wine with rich lemon fruit, we're seeing more of it on wine lists these days because it's crisp and usually quite ballsy for a white wine. This tastes at its best when it's young and fridge-cold.

Fiano & Carricante 👁
SICILY

Sicily's answer to fruity white wine comes from the local Fiano grape. It's easy to say, and easy to drink, because it can taste of lemons or apples. Carricante is one to watch and comes from the region around Mount Etna – it's chewy with ripe lemon and tangy orange flavours.

Arneis *Say it: arr-nay-iss* ⭐
PIEDMONT

I have a serious crush on this grape. Why? Because it has never failed to deliver crisp, peachy fruit with a hint of almond, and sometimes a squeeze of orange, too. Its home is in the Roero sub-region of Piedmont, and is often called 'Roero Arneis' on wine lists. It makes a delicious white wine with attitude but it should be drunk young-ish; the best ones I've enjoyed were two to three years old.

Pecorino
MARCHE

This is an easy-drinking, mild-flavoured grape native to central Italy. Quality can vary, but overall I've found it to be crisp and always more complex than Pinot Grigio.

Ribolla Gialla *Say it: ree-bolla jar-la*
FRIULI

Very nutty and waxy in flavour and usually a deep-golden colour. This is a food white for me – the flavour is strong and it often has a chewy texture.

Friulano
FRIULI

Floral, juicy, pretty and perky, there's a lot to be said for a glass of chilled Friulano on a hot summer's day. Not much of it is made but it's always been a winner in my book.

Vermentino
TUSCANY & SARDINIA

Thanks to Chianti, Tuscany is red wine country for most people. But the coast of Tuscany makes some blisteringly cool and crisp whites from the Vermentino grape (known as Rolle in the south of France). Its prolific in Sardinia, too; in fact, it's the signature white grape of this island. Salty, crisp and full of lemon flavour, it's a no-brainer with a simple grilled fish dish.

Verdicchio *Say it: vair-deek-ee-yo*
MARCHE

One of the better known of Italy's local grapes, Verdicchio is found all over Italy, but its most famous Italian home is in the region of Marche. Like many of its native Italian siblings, it's lemon-fresh and has that citrus and almond combination of flavour, although it's often accompanied by a crisp acid character.

spanish whites

There's much more to Spanish white wine than Albariño, as delicious as that can be. It's easy to think of Spain just as a hot country that's great for punchy reds, but it's a mountainous and coastal one, too, and these areas have cool enough conditions for perky white wines to be made as well. In fact, in the last 15 years or so, there's been a huge transformation in Spanish white wines, with a greater focus on zesty, fruity whites. The change in the Spanish white wine scene is (a bit like Italy's) thanks to an improvement in technology that has allowed producers to make the most of high-quality local grape varieties.

Verdejo *Say it: ver-dec-koh*
RUEDA *Say it: roo-ay-dah*

Verdejo is one of the new darling white wines by-the-glass in restaurants and bars. It's most famously made in the northern Spanish region of Rueda, but it's also one of the most widely planted white grapes in the country. At its best it has a really intense aroma of flowers and nuts, especially almonds (almond is a common flavour note for many Spanish whites), while in the mouth it can be crisp but juicy. Sometimes it's blended with Sauvignon Blanc, and this makes it taste even more herbaceous. But you can also find oak-aged Verdejo, and when it's spent time in barrel, those nutty flavours really come into their own.

Albariño *Say it: al-bar-een-yo*
RÍAS BAIXAS *Say it: ree-as baish-as*

A perennially popular Spanish white grape that's known very well internationally, Albariño makes your quintessential coastal white wine, grown in Rías Baixas in Galicia, the coastal part of Spain that sits just above Portugal. It's in its element when paired with seafood. Albariño is all about a floral, zesty, citrus-flavoured white with a lick of sea-air saltiness, which is the secret to its fantastic match with fish and shellfish. These wines are made to be drunk young, while they're at their freshest, although there are always a few producers who are experimenting with different styles of 'classic' Albariño by using oak and mixing in other grape varieties that may help it age. Pazo de Señorans makes some seriously top-end Albariño, while Martín Códax's wines are also worth checking out.

Godello
VALDEORRAS ★

It's hard not to be seduced by the story of a grape on the verge of extinction being revived, and not just being revived, but also making delicious wine. North of the Portuguese border, the little-known region of Valdeorras has made big waves with Godello in the last 25 years. Today it makes very sunny wines full of fleshy peach flavours, but also with a cool and crisp edge to them. Godello is highly thought of among those in-the-know, and has enough oomph and depth to stand up to time with oak (if that's the style producers want – a Godello with extra structure to age for a bit longer). If you're into luscious apple, nutty, developed flavours in your wine, give older Godello a try. Check out the wines of Rafael Palacios – these are nothing short of gorgeous!

Viura
RIOJA

White Rioja's thunder is always stolen by red Rioja, which is a bit of a shame because the whites of this landlocked region of northern Spain can be very good. Like its red counterpart, white Rioja is usually made from a blend of grapes, except that in white Rioja, Viura is the star; with the red, it's the grape Tempranillo.

White Rioja has a traditional, loyal following, but I've got to admit that young white Rioja has never really set my heart racing, mostly because it doesn't seem to have as much flavour or personality as other Spanish whites. When young, it's fresh and crisp, but there's no overwhelming Viura flavour per se.

Some sommeliers, though, love a barrel-fermented Viura-based white Rioja because it can be very complex and have a waxy texture and flavour that is great for food. However, production of this style is on the decrease – it's become a casualty of Spain's white wine revolution because producers are concentrating on making light and zesty whites instead.

The producer Muga has a good reputation in Rioja and makes a good midway, everyday Viura-based white Rioja; it's been barrel-fermented but still tastes of melon fruit rather than wood. Typically, Viura is blended with Garnacha Blanca and Malvasia to make white Rioja, but I prefer Viura when it's used to make Cava, and it's actually one of the more popular grapes used in making Spain's leading sparkling wine. A common synonym for Viura is Macabeo, by the way.

Have you heard of Airén?

It's the most widely planted grape variety in Spain, although red grapes Tempranillo and Cabernet Sauvignon are now giving it a run for its money. That said, I wouldn't search too hard for a table wine made from this. It's mostly used in the production of Spanish brandy. Let's hope it stays that way!

Garnacha Blanca
ALL ACROSS SPAIN

Yes, Garnacha comes in white as well as red (and pink too, if anyone's asking!). Garnacha Blanca is found in various pockets of Spain, and most of those are in the north. Known as Grenache Blanc in France, it generally doesn't produce a wine that's going to rock the world by itself, as it isn't especially refined or classy. However, it does have its uses, especially in blended wines, where it can either boost the alcohol content or richen the body of a wimpy white.

One of Garnacha Blanca's most famous appearances is in white Rioja, although as I say above, Viura usually takes the lead role for white wines here.

Hondarrabi Zuri
CHACOLÍ/TXAKOLI *Say it: chak-oh-lee*

This one sounds a little bit crazy I know, that's because it's the local Basque name given to the most important grape in the region – and wine style – of Txakoli. Txakoli is also what you're more likely to see on the label, rather than this grape name.

Not much of it is made by Spanish winemaking standards, but its quality and production have improved considerably in the last 20 years. It makes crunchy white wines that taste of green apples and I love it for being incredibly fresh and zingy. The producer Txomín Etxaníz *(say it: cho-min etch-anith)* makes some lovely wines in this pretty Spanish spot. Oh, and in French Basque country, this grape is known as Courbu Blanc.

Malvasia
LANZAROTE

Last year a Spanish sommelier friend of mine tipped the Canary Islands as a region to watch, and having since tasted some of the wines, I agree. Red wines probably rule here, but when Malvasia is done well it's really delicious, especially in Lanzarote, where the volcanic soils give a savoury, earthy edge to the apple-flavoured fruit.

Macabeo/Xarello/Parellada (Cava)
PENEDÈS, CATALONIA

Cava is Spain's signature sparkling wine. It's a style name, though, rather than a region as most people think, and in fact can be made in a number of different Spanish locations. That said, the engine room of Cava is in Penedès in Catalonia, just west of Barcelona.

Cava has shared the limelight with Prosecco in recent years, as the recessionary 'alternative' sparkling wine to Champagne because it's typically more affordable. But the Cava scene is changing as we speak and the style is trying to make more serious wines.

You can see this change in the grape varieties being used. Cava used to be made of very local Spanish grapes like Macabeo, Xarrello and Parellada, and although these are still widely planted and used,

the authorities have given winemakers permission to use Chardonnay and Pinot Noir in the wines. This has been significant in improving the quality of the traditionally appley-flavoured Cava, making some of it more complex and able to age.

Macabeo (Viura) I talk about on the opposite page, but as for the other two native Cava grapes, Xarello is the most revered, and its reputation is better than that of Parellada because it has some oomph and guts to its flavour, together with a powerful freshness, which can be useful in the Spanish heat. For all the buzz about Chardonnay and Pinot Noir on today's Cava scene, some producers still prefer to stay very local, and one producer whose wines show the best of the local Xarello grape is Gramona, so track it down if you can. As for Parellada, this grape's most useful job in Cava is to make the wine smell floral.

PICK THE RIGHT WINE:
FORTIFIED, SWEET & FIZZ

Whether you know the grape you want, the flavour you are in the mood for, or the food you're eating, we all need a little shortcut at some point in our lives, so this is a quick reference guide for when it's that kind of moment.

fortified

Younger Sherry & younger Madeira → salty · citrus

Older Sherry & older Madeira → caramel · nuts

} game
spicy food
tapas

Pedro Ximénez Sherry → liquorice · prune

Red Port → fruit cake · fig

Tawny Port → dried fruit · toffee

White Port → citrus · herbaceous

Marsala → fig · nuts

Rutherglen Muscat → prune · leather

} aperitif
chocolate
dessert

sweet

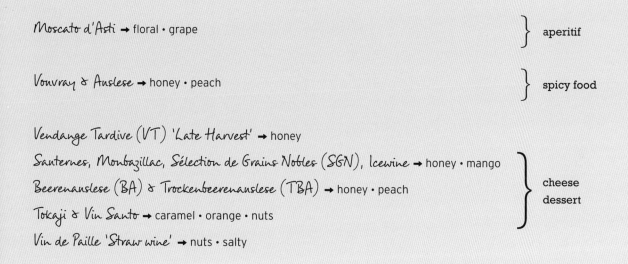

Moscato d'Asti ➡ floral · grape ⎫ aperitif

Vouvray & Auslese ➡ honey · peach ⎫ spicy food

Vendange Tardive (VT) 'Late Harvest' ➡ honey
Santernes, Monbazillac, Sélection de Grains Nobles (SGN), Icewine ➡ honey · mango
Beerenauslese (BA) & Trockenbeerenauslese (TBA) ➡ honey · peach ⎫ cheese
Tokaji & Vin Santo ➡ caramel · orange · nuts   dessert
Vin de Paille 'Straw wine' ➡ nuts · salty

fizz

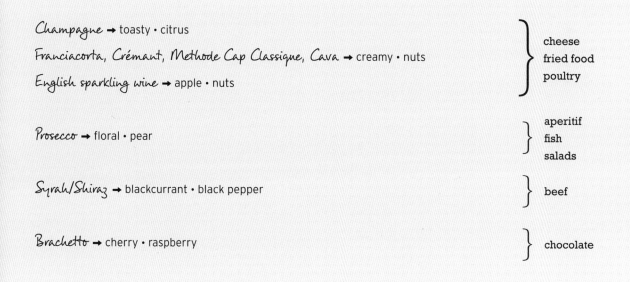

Champagne ➡ toasty · citrus
Franciacorta, Crémant, Methode Cap Classique, Cava ➡ creamy · nuts ⎫ cheese / fried food / poultry
English sparkling wine ➡ apple · nuts

Prosecco ➡ floral · pear ⎫ aperitif / fish / salads

Syrah/Shiraz ➡ blackcurrant · black pepper ⎫ beef

Brachetto ➡ cherry · raspberry ⎫ chocolate

fortified

What I really hope is that you're not just reading this page for one of these reasons: it's winter or Christmas, you want an after-dinner drink or you want a wine to go with dessert. Fortified wines are great for all these occasions, sure, but they also have a lot more to offer. They can be refreshing wines for any time of the year, many of them are gorgeous as an aperitif, and some can even pair their way through an entire meal. However, those people who freak out at the mention of fortified wine, or refuse even to let it pass their lips, usually act like this because: they think it's all sweet – it's not; they think it all tastes 'spirity' – it doesn't; or people get drunk after just one glass – they don't (although that depends on the size of the glass!).

Fortified wine starts life in the winery like any normal table wine. Then it gets fortified. This involves adding a dollop of neutral-flavoured grape spirit to the wine, which doesn't change the flavour but does boost the alcohol level. Fortifying the wine is also the reason why many of them are sweet as well, because often the spirit is added to the wine before it's finished its conversion of sugar to alcohol (the fermentation process), and when there's a high level of leftover sugar in a wine, it's going to end up sweet.

Fortified wine is made all over the world, but there are three famous types: Port, Sherry and Madeira. We'll explore all of these here, as well as a few others that are lesser-known but are definitely worth drinking and knowing about. For the quality of the wine inside the bottle, fortified wines can be incredibly good value for money.

Port

The name of Port is protected, so there's no such thing as 'Australian Port' or 'French Port', for example. It has to come from the Douro Valley in Portugal – one of the most achingly beautiful wine regions in the world. Port can be white, pink or red, and most of it is sweet.

The Douro Valley is in northern Portugal, east of Oporto. Portugal is such a hotbed of native grapes, there can be as many as 80 different ones used in a red Port, but of these, here are the key and most common ones.

Touriga Nacional
This is the jewel in the Port crown and makes a wine with a concentrated and unique aroma, a deep colour and rich tannins.

Tinta Roriz
Also known as Tempranillo in Spain, this often gives a leathery flavour to the wine and can be high in alcohol with rich fruit flavour and tannins.

Touriga Franca
Popular for its floral aroma and deep colour, it's rich, but it's not as intense in flavour as one of its parents, Touriga Nacional.

Tinta Barroca
This can give a savoury, earthy flavour to the wine. It has very dark skins that makes the wine very dark, too.

Tinta Cão
This is spicy and likes the cooler vineyard posts so it retains its lovely violet, floral aroma.

Port ranges in colour and is transformed into many different styles – the main ones, and their general characteristics are outlined below.

WHITE
This can be dry or sweet. It's made like a red Port, just using white grapes like Rabigato and Codega. White Port and tonic is a hugely popular long-drink aperitif in Portugal and is heavenly with toasted almonds.

PINK
A relatively new Port style, created by the Port house Taylor's but now made by several producers. This is an aperitif wine, really, and should be served chilled like White Port. It is also great in a summer cocktail (see page 87).

RUBY
The lightest and simplest style of red Port, it's sweet, made from a blend of different years and should be drunk as soon as it's bought, within 2–3 days once open.

TAWNY
A massively underrated wine, Tawny Port is aged for a long time in barrels. This contact with wood has made the Port turn a brown colour, hence the name. It's sweet and often tastes of oranges, nuts and toffee, and is delicious as a chilled aperitif or with desserts where orange, vanilla or nuts are key ingredients. Aged Tawny comes in a mix of years and you can gauge intensity by its average age on the label.

COLHEITA
This is a more intensely flavoured version of Tawny Port, made from a single year.

VINTAGE
The pinnacle of Port production. Vintage Ports are only released in years the producers really rate. These are very serious wines that need to be stored laid down and are not for early drinking. They throw a sediment and therefore need decanting, and have an intense flavour that is mellow, rich, and full of fruit cake flavour that lasts for a long time.

LBV
'Late Bottled Vintage' is a great value-for-money wine and is especially good because it has all the richness and fruit of Vintage Port but without the hassle of decanting it. This is a Port that comes from one year, but it's spent more time in wood than Vintage Port, which softens it more quickly and therefore it can be drunk earlier. Although most LBV doesn't need decanting, if it says Traditional LBV on the label, it will.

SINGLE QUINTA
If a year's harvest is thought to be of very good quality but not quite good enough to declare it 'Vintage', then Port houses will make a wine from a particular plot (*quinta*) on their property. This is great as an after-dinner digestif – perfect for chocolate.

Declaring a Vintage Port

In the wine community, 'declaring' a vintage Port is a big deal. It happens when Port houses deem the year to be of exceptional quality, although each house can make this declaration independently. On average, a Vintage Port is declared about three times a decade.

Sherry

Like Port, the name of Sherry is protected. There's no such thing as an 'Italian Sherry' or a 'Californian Sherry', for example. It has to come from Andalucía in south-west Spain and the word 'Sherry' is actually an English derivation of the place it comes from, Jerez. Sherry is going through a popularity renaissance at the moment and it can be bone-dry or sweet and can range in colour from almost colourless to deep, opaque mahogany. For more on Sherry, see page 121.

Palomino Fino

The most planted grape in the region of Jerez by a long way, Palomino Fino makes all of the dry sherries and is the base of many sherries that end up being sweet, too. By nature, it's a neutral-flavoured grape. The flavour you get in Sherry comes from its ageing process, not the grape's flavour.

Pedro Ximénez

This is usually referred to just by its initials: PX. On its own, it makes an intensely sweet wine that's an opaque brown colour, and tastes of liquorice and vanilla.

Moscatel

A grape commonly used to make sweet wines in Spain, it's only ever used to make a sweet Sherry, or, like with PX, to sweeten an existing dry Sherry (made with Palomino Fino).

The ageing process of Sherry in *bodegas* (the wineries where Sherry is made) is integral to how it tastes. There are two ways of ageing a Sherry; biologically and oxidatively. Biological ageing is for fino, manzanilla and amontillado. This involves a yeast layer called 'flor', forming on top of the wine in the barrel to stop contact with the air and limit oxidization so the wine stays fresh. This gives the Sherry a very yeasty, bready flavour. Fino and manzanilla are in the barrel for shortest time, so they taste younger and are always dry. When the flor dies away and the wine oxidizes, these wines turn into amontillado. Oxidative ageing, as the name suggests, is the ageing process where Sherries have no flor in the barrel. The longer a Sherry ages in barrel, the more intense its flavour and the more alcoholic it will become, because as the water in the wine evaporates, the ratio of alcohol to liquid increases.

FINO & MANZANILLA *Say it: fee-no and man-tha-nee-ya*
Both these styles are always completely dry, and are the lightest in alcohol of all Sherries. They're fresh and have a salty, appetite-whetting flavour, so should be drunk fridge-cold. On a hot day, these make an unbeatable zesty aperitif.

AMONTILLADO *Say it: ah-mon-tee-yar-doh*
A step up in richness from fino and manzanilla, this style is usually aged for longer before it's released. It tastes of lightly toasted nuts and has a tangy orange flavour. Most of it is dry, but some is sweet, so check the label. A dry one is great with griddled octopus or cured ham.

PALO CORTADO *Say it: pah-lo cor-tah-do*
For me, this is the most versatile of Sherry styles. It's a step up in richness from amontillado; in fact it's often described as having the nose of amontillado and the palate of oloroso. Here, the flavour has caramelized nuts with the freshness of orange and a rich vanilla spice. A dry one is delicious with something like a chicken tagine with prunes and figs, while a sweeter version is perfect with a spiced carrot cake.

OLOROSO *Say it: oll-oh-rosso*
The richest of the dry Sherries, and the one that will have been aged for longest. Oloroso tastes of figs,

prunes and liquorice, but it can also be dry or sweet, and both are heavenly. Dry oloroso can be great with the gamey flavours of guinea fowl, and the sweeter kind is a mellow, rich drink to have after dinner.

PEDRO XIMÉNEZ

This is for people with a sweet tooth, is intensely dark in colour and at its best when poured over vanilla ice cream.

Madeira

The Portuguese island of Madeira is also the name given to its fortified wine. I think this is the most misunderstood of all fortified wines, yet it's also one of the easiest to understand, because the grape variety dictates the level of sweetness. What's incredible about Madeira is the length of time it can age. These wines can go up to 100 years and still taste amazingly fresh, plus they can last a long time once opened without disappearing – and I'm talking weeks, sometimes months. It's robust but incredibly sensual, all of which makes Madeira ridiculously good value for money.

Sercial

A dry wine with a tangy orange flavour, it has a smoky tobacco taste and good richness, even though it's dry.

Verdelho

As a grape it's the most planted on the island. Off-dry as a wine, it tastes of dried apricots and honey, and is delicious with hard cheeses.

Bual/Boal

Medium-sweet as a wine, it's famous for having an incredible perfume of caramel and orange – boiled sweets/hard candy is a common flavour description, and an accurate one.

Malvasia/Malmsey

This is the sweetest Madeira – it's dark brown in colour and tastes of toffee apples, caramelized pineapple and caramelized nuts. Heavenly.

More fortified wine
VIN DOUX NATUREL

As it translates, this is a 'naturally sweet wine', because of the sugar left in the wine after the fermentation has been stopped. It's a speciality of the south of France, but it's not exclusive to this area. Some of the most common VDNs include Rivesaltes, Muscat, Maury, Banyuls and Samos (see pages 96–99), and smell of orange blossom and have a caramelized orange flavour on the palate – heady stuff. Rivesaltes from France can be white or red, while Muscat de Rivesaltes has a pretty elderflower flavour, but is not as revered as Muscat de Beaumes-de-Venise.

Maurys from French Roussillon are made with Grenache Noir. Although sweet and fortified, these red wines can be rich in tannin so need some time to age and mellow, but they're delicious with chocolate.

Rutherglen in Victoria, Australia, is the most famous fortified wine region in Australia and Muscat is the jewel in its crown. Vines here are extremely old and many date back to the gold rush period of the 1850s. These sweet fortified wines are dark brown in colour and extremely intense after their very long period of ageing in barrels. They often smell and taste of crème brûlée, caramelized nuts, butterscotch, caramel and treacle/molasses. These make a brilliant match with a nutty, chocolate dessert.

Sherry

Haven't you heard? Sherry is going through a renaissance. Seriously, right now it's the must-have drink in some of the world's coolest cities. The popularity of tapas especially has brought Sherry to the front of the wine list because it has a natural affinity with this style of food. For wine-lovers already wise to Sherry's deliciousness, the whole Sherry scene is extra-exciting at the moment because the bodegas keep coming up with innovative, quirky and limited-edition wines, and these really transport you back to its home in south-west Spain. The renaissance hasn't caught up with everyone just yet, though, and too many Sherry urban myths still exist, so let's tackle these right here, right now.

Urban myth 1: It's all sweet
Forget what's in Grandma's cupboard, a lot of the best Sherry is dry. Like, D-R-Y. In fact, styles like fino and manzanilla are often drier than your average glass of Sauvignon Blanc or Chardonnay.

Urban myth 2: It's all grey and gloopy
Cream Sherry is the thick, sweet Sherry that most people associate with all Sherry, but this is just one style of Sherry, and not the most exciting one, either. Cream Sherry is usually a blend of different sherries that have been deliberately sweetened and coloured. Sherry can range from being clear and pale lemon in colour to light caramel or dark mahogany.

Urban myth 3: It can be made anywhere
Sherry can only be called Sherry if it comes from its designated region in south-west Spain. In other words, there's no such thing as 'Australian Sherry' or 'South African Sherry' or 'French Sherry', etc.

Urban myth 4: It can be kept for years
Please don't keep your Sherry for years. Especially if it's been opened. A fino or manzanilla should be treated like a white wine – keep it for a maximum of two days once opened, preferably in the fridge. The other richer styles shouldn't really be kept for more than a week or two, either.

Urban myth 5: It's too strong
Sherry is a fortified wine, sure, but it can still make some incredibly refreshing wines. The lightest styles, fino and manzanilla, are usually around 15% ABV (alcohol by volume) and taste zingy on the palate. These days you can find many unfortified wines that are just as high in alcohol.

Urban myth 6: It's red
It's a common mistake to make, but it is impossible to make red Sherry – it's only ever made from white grapes.

Urban myth 7: All Sherry is ageless
Most Sherry is given an average age because it's made of a blend of sherries from different years, but you can still find sherries from one year. They are rare and special, and usually delicious because a bodega will only have released a 'vintage' Sherry if it is confident in the wine from that year.

Urban myth 8: It's only for before dinner
Sherry is one of the most versatile wines around, which means there are styles for before, during and after a meal.

sweet

When it comes to unfortified sweet wines, classics like Sauternes hog the limelight while German Riesling (unfairly) gets a pretty bad rap. There are actually many styles and grapes used to make sweet wine, although it's true that certain grape varieties lend themselves to making sweet wines better than others. These include Sauvignon Blanc, Muscat, Semillon, Riesling and Gewürztraminer, so you'll see these grapes pop up time and again to make sweet wines all over the word. Often but not always, sweet wines are lower in alcohol, too, because there's too much sugar in the wine for the alcohol fermentation to keep going. They are called many things, including 'dessert wines', although this isn't a favourite of mine as it implies that they're only good for desserts, which isn't true! They're also nicknamed 'sticky wines' and this itself is often shortened to 'stickies'. In the UK, they're often referred to as 'pudding wines', too.

Unfortified sweet wines can be split into four categories, as well as four styles: delicate and floral whites, rich and honeyed whites, sparkling, and red. Below are the most common methods of making sweet wine, and all of them involve having a grape that's high in sugar before the grape juice goes through fermentation to turn into wine.

LATE HARVEST (VENDANGE TARDIVE – VT)
The grapes are deliberately harvested late so the sugar continues to accumulate as the grape hangs on the vine.

BOTRYTIS ('NOBLE ROT')
When grapes are infected with a good rot called *Botrytis cinerea*, they shrivel up as the water evaporates, leaving a high proportion of sugar.

ICEWINE (EISWEIN)
Wine made from grapes that freeze on the vine. When extracting the juice from the grape, the water is frozen, leaving the grape high in sugar.

STRAW WINE
After the grapes are harvested, they're left on mats (often made of straw) to dehydrate, again leaving a high proportion of sugar.

France
SAUTERNES & BARSAC, BORDEAUX
These are the most famous sweet wines in the world. Sauternes, and within it Barsac, uses three grapes to make sweet wine: Sauvignon Blanc, Semillon and Muscadelle. They are rich, very honeyed and taste of exotic fruits like mango, but also of orange and nuts. One of the most famous sweet wines in the world is Château d'Yquem, although I like Château Suduiraut.

ALSACE
The most common grapes for sweet wine in Alsace are Riesling, Gewurztraminer and Muscat, although these grapes also make excellent dry wines here. Look at the label to tell the difference, if it says 'Vendange Tardive' (VT) or 'Sélection de Grains Nobles' (SGN), the wine will be sweet.

COTEAUX DU LAYON, LOIRE VALLEY
The honeyed white that tastes of candied citrus from this region is underrated and fairly unknown. It's a delicate sweet wine made from Chenin Blanc grapes in the Anjou section of the Loire Valley where the three most respected sub-regions are Bonnezeaux, Quarts-de-Chaume and Coteaux du Layon.

VOUVRAY, LOIRE VALLEY

Vouvray is in the Touraine part of the Loire Valley, and makes delicate and floral, still or sparkling, as well as dry, off-dry, medium and sweet wines, so it's really worth checking the label properly. The reason the style can vary so much is that the region can't always guarantee its grapes will be sweet enough to make a full-on sweet wine. Like Coteaux du Layon, Vouvray is made from the Loire's signature white grape, Chenin Blanc.

MONBAZILLAC, SOUTH-WEST FRANCE

Often (and rightly) billed as a wallet-friendly alternative to Sauternes and Barsac, these honeyed whites are made from Sauvignon Blanc, Semillon and Musacdelle.

JURANÇON, SOUTH-WEST FRANCE

These wines, from the Basque corner of France, are a real feather in France's winemaking cap. They fall under two sweetness levels, simply called Jurançon, which is incredibly sweet, or Jurançon Vendange Tardives, which is even sweeter. They are usually made from the Petit Manseng or Gros Manseng grapes, and they taste of caramel, honeysuckle, exotic fruits and vanilla.

PACHERENC DU VIC-BILH, MADIRAN ⭐

Dry and sweet white wines made in Madiran have to be called Pacherenc but can drop the du Vic-Bilh. The sweet wines are usually late-harvest wines made from local grapes or Petit Manseng and Petit Courbu.

VIN DE PAILLE, JURA

Jura is France's smallest winemaking region, found east of Burgundy, and its speciality sweet wine is Vin de Paille, a straw wine. Vin de Paille is made from Chardonnay, Savagnin, Poulsard, and sometimes another local grape called Trousseau. It can come in different levels of sweetness, from medium to full-on tooth-tinglingly sweet.

Hungary

TOKAJI *Say it: tock-eye*

Hungary's most famous wine and one of the most famous sweet wines in the world. Tokaji the wine comes from Tokaj the region (the 'i' differentiates the wine from the place) and is made with Furmint grapes, native to Hungary. It's heavenly, rich in caramel, toffee and dried-apricot flavour, and can be expensive.

Italy

VIN SANTO, TUSCANY

This is a sweet straw wine mainly made from two white grapes: Trebbiano Toscana and Malvasia Bianco. After harvest, the grapes are laid out on mats or hung up to air-dry from the ceiling. They usually have a rich amber colour, which comes from ageing in large wooden barrels and make a rich and nutty nectar.

MOSCATO D'ASTI, PIEDMONT

Light and fizzy, this pretty Moscato is often my go-to sweet wine at the end of a meal because it's low in alcohol, around 5.5% ABV (alcohol by volume), and very refreshing, too. Moscato d'Asti often gets confused with the inferior Asti, which is much sweeter and the bubbles are larger so it tastes more fizzy.

PASSITO DEL PANTELLERIA, SICILY

Pantelleria is a satellite island off Sicily and *Passito* is the Italian name given to dried-out grapes. Just 50 miles from Tunisia, it's super-hot here. Moscato, is the grape used for this style – it's unctuous and very honeyed.

RECIOTO DELLA VALPOLICELLA & VALPOLICELLA RIPASSO, VENETO

Recioto is a delicious sweet red wine made in

Valpolicella. It can be still or slightly sparkling and is made using Corvina, Rondinella and Molinara grapes. Valpolicella Ripasso is the wine made from the dried red grape skins that are used in making the Recioto.

Germany

Riesling is king in Germany, as we know. Its sweet wines are usually made from Riesling, following a general hierachy of sweetness, although if the label says 'Trocken' this is a guarantee that the wines are dry.

SPÄTLESE

Translated, this means 'late-picked', but the cool thing to do at the moment is to make dry wines with these grapes, even though they are late-picked, so it can be a gamble. Dry or sweet, the wines have a floral, honeyed character, and are great with spicy Asian dishes.

AUSLESE

Meaning 'select' wines, these grapes hang on the vines until they're deemed sweet enough, so mainly they're late harvest but sometimes they will have botrytis-affected grapes in them, too. They have a tight acidity and rounded honeyed character.

BEERENAUSLESE (BA) & TROCKENBEERENAUSLESE (TBA)

Made only from botrytis-affected grapes to make Rieslings that are pure and full of life. TBA is a step up in sweetness from BA. It's super-concentrated, super-intense, super-sweet.

EISWEIN (ICEWINE)

Very concentrated, and with such full-on acidity that the wines will age for many years.

Austria

Austria's sweet-wine hierarchy and vocabulary is influenced by Germany – from Spätlese to Eiswein – but it also has a couple of its own speciality sweet wines. These are also usually made from Riesling.

STROHWEIN, BURGENLAND

As you might have guessed from the name, this is Austria's version of straw wine and the rules say the grapes must be laid out on straw mats or hung up to air-dry for a minimum of three months to dehydrate. They make honeyed, sweet wines.

AUSBRUCH, BURGENLAND

Ausbruch is a wine made with botrytis-affected grapes and has a strict minimum sugar-level stipulation as well as a strict origin. It's a speciality from the town of Rust, which means it can only come from there.

USA, New Zealand, Australia & Chile

All of these countries make sweet wines from a variety of grapes. Relaxed winemaking laws mean anything is possible, so they can be made from any grapes in any place, although the most popular ones tend to be made from Semillon, Riesling, Muscat and Sauvignon Blanc.

South Africa

Chenin Blanc is often made into a dessert wine in the straw-wine method here. A few standout producers are Mullineux and De Trafford.

Canada

Icewine is Canada's speciality, and Riesling is the grape that makes the most exquisite wines, but the Vidal grape is also widely used. This honeyed nectar usually has a fantastic freshness.

fizz

We sparkling-wine drinkers have never had it so good. While Champagne, Cava and Prosecco make up the most famous fizzy trio on the planet, today the world is bursting with classic, experimental and funky sparkling wines, any of which can be young or old, spritzy or fizzy, dry or sweet, white, rosé or red (yes, red).

The fizz

Firstly, let's get to grips with how the bubbles are locked into wine because it's a pretty major component in what the final wine will look like.

TRADITIONAL (CHAMPAGNE) METHOD

This is the most expensive method and it's widely thought to make the highest-quality sparkling wine, complex enough to age. Here, the second fermentation takes place inside the bottle and the carbon dioxide created by that fermentation dissolves into the wine, making it fizzy. However, the second fermentation isn't just important for the bubbles; it also produces a deposit that's made up of dead yeast cells, called 'lees'.

Traditional-method wines have to be aged 'on the lees' for a minimum period of time, depending on the style and where it's made. Resting on the lees gives the wine extra flavour and complexity, and can make the wine taste more like bread, which is easy to understand because the lees is yeast. Some regions stipulate this method *must* be used in order for the wine to call itself that particular wine style. These include Cava and Champagne, as well as Franciacorta in Italy, Crémant in France and Methode Cap Classique in South Africa. And although most English sparkling wine is also made this way, there's no requirement that it has to be.

TRANSFER METHOD

This is useful for sparkling wines that are made in large quantities, or wines that will be sold in very large bottles. Here, the wine also goes through a second fermentation in the bottle. After this, it is transferred to a large vat so it can be filtered, then it's rebottled, but there's always the risk that some bubbles get lost between transfers.

TANK (CHARMAT) METHOD

This is good for sparkling wines that are made from aromatic grapes and for early drinking, and that's why it's used for Prosecco, which is made from the floral Glera grape. It involves a second fermentation taking place in a large tank, then transferring the wine into bottles under pressure.

CARBONATION

This method is used for wines that are made for immediate drinking. Here, a still table wine is simply injected with carbon dioxide: a bit like how you would use a Soda Stream.

The grapes

Any grapes can make a sparkling wine. They vary from being very local and relatively unknown to international grapes like Pinot Noir and Chardonnay, which are the two universally admired and thought to make the best sparkling wine. A good number of the best sparkling wines are made from grapes grown in cooler climates because the natural high acidity in these grapes is the perfect starting point before the wine goes through the enrichening processes involved in making it sparkling.

fizz: styles, regions & flavours

BRUT NV

The flagship sparkling wine style. 'Brut' means 'dry' and 'NV' means 'non-vintage', or not from one specific year. Certain producers prefer multi-vintage, where you'll see 'MV' on the label. For this style, older wines will have deliberately been kept in the winery, waiting to be blended. Pulling all these different years together is important, because it ensures the wine tastes the same from year to year – and we wine drinkers have an unspoken deal that there is a house 'style' that tastes the same, day in, day out.

ROSÉ

The double-whammy of popularity at the moment – sparkling *and* pink wine – so no wonder sales of pink fizz go from strength to strength. See pages 66–69 to see how fizz is made pink.

BRUT ZERO, BRUT NATURE, ZERO DOSAGE

An intensely dry sparkling wine that's very popular right now. The sweetness level of sparkling wine is determined halfway through its production process, when a little topping-up liquid known as liqueur de tirage determines how sweet the final wine will be. If you add no sugar to the wine, it falls into the 'Brut Zero' category, which purists love because the wine isn't masked by any sugar.

BLANC DE BLANCS

A fizz made only from white grapes, typically Chardonnay, which is the only main white grape in Champagne, but most places that make a Chardonnay-only sparkling wine will refer to it as a Blanc de Blancs anyway. This is the ultimate crisp and elegant aperitif.

BLANC DE NOIRS

A fizz only made from red grapes, which usually means they're made from Pinot Noir or Pinot Meunier, or both. Again, the influence is Champagne. They make fuller sparkling wines than Blanc de Blancs, with more red-fruit richness.

VINTAGE

A sparkling wine from one year. Vintage Champagnes are usually very good value for money, even if they're more expensive than Brut NV. In Champagne, they'll usually only release a vintage if the year is thought to be great. Vintage wines are more common in newer sparkling wine because they don't have older wines to make a NV.

PRESTIGE CUVÉE

The crème de la crème, they command high prices. Examples of Champagne prestige cuvées include Crystal, Belle Époque, Comtes de Champagne, R.D., Cuvée Sir Winston Churchill, Krug and Dom Pérignon.

CHAMPAGNE, FRANCE

The benchmark sparkling wine for most people. Champagne is from Champagne, in north-east France; everything made outside of Champagne is sparkling wine. Whatever the style, grape or age of Champagne, it's synonymous with elegance and complexity, because it's fruity but toasty and has many layers of flavour. Champagne is made using the traditional method, and typically from three grapes: Pinot Noir and Pinot Meunier (both red), and Chardonnay (white). It's a great wine to pair with food and can work throughout a meal.

CRÉMANT, FRANCE

Crémant can provide serious value for money. It's the name given to quality French sparkling wines that aren't from the Champagne region. They are made in the traditional method and come from many different regions using local grapes.

PROSECCO, ITALY
Prosecco is a region in north-east Italy. Made from the Glera grape in the tank method, it's perky and fruity.

FRANCIACORTA, ITALY
Italy's equivalent to Champagne is a delicious toasty sparkling wine with serious elegance. Franciacorta is the name of the region and the wine style. Its home is Lombardy, and it is largely made up from Chardonnay and Pinot Nero (Noir), and sometimes Pinot Bianco (Blanc), too. Satèn is a gorgeous Franciacorta style that's silky-smooth in texture, because it has a lower atmospheric pressure than other fizz. Two lovely producers are Fratelli Berlucchi and Bellavista.

METHODE CAP CLASSIQUE, SOUTH AFRICA
The quality sparkling wine from South Africa is often shortened to 'MCC'. Usually made from Sauvignon Blanc, Chenin Blanc, Chardonnay or Pinot Noir, these are flavourful wines made in the traditional method and improving all the time. Graham Beck and Villiera make good ones.

SPARKLING SHIRAZ, AUSTRALIA
Australian and drunk at Christmas to go with the myriad of flavours on the table (or barbecue). It has the classic juicy black fruit of Shiraz with black pepper, pepped up with bubbles. Seppelt, Peter Lehman and Jacob's Creek all make juicy versions of this red fizz.

TASMANIA, AUSTRALIA
The hub of quality sparkling wine out of Australia, the conditions in Tasmania are cool enough to give the grapes (often Chardonnay and Pinot Noir) the best possible chance of being made into a crisp and fresh sparkling wine. Jansz makes great value-for-money ones.

ENGLAND
In the last decade or so, the English sparkling wine scene has exploded, with new wines and producers coming out all the time because England has the perfect conditions for Chardonnay and Pinot Noir, the two leading sparkling wine grapes. English fizz has a distinctive apple character. Nyetimber and Ridgeview are the pioneers, but I also like Coates & Seely, Gusbourne and Jenkyn Place.

CALIFORNIA, USA
California is making great quality sparkling wine. In fact, there's been a lot of investment from Champagne houses here. These wines are usually made with Pinot Noir and Chardonnay, and are usually very toasty and buttery.

Brazil: the wildcard
This is no new-fangled craze. Brazilian sparkling wine actually celebrates 100 years of production in 2015. As in California, not much is exported, but the quality is improving all the time. Most comes from Serra Gaúcha, its most important winemaking region, found right on the southern tip of the country.

the
table

Wine takes on a whole new meaning when it's served with food. Our senses get distracted and our taste buds start a new journey. Wine with food is a flexible process; there are commonsense paths to follow based on the characteristics of certain wines and ingredients, but there isn't always one definitive wine for one definitive food. That's why matching the two is always so exciting.

meat

The number of wines that work with meat probably matches the number of meat dishes that exist – an infinite number! Having said that, there are certain grapes and wine styles that work time and again with different meat dishes. These wines, like Beaujolais or the grapes Pinot Noir and Syrah/Shiraz are so versatile with meat that it's always worth having one or two of them stashed away.

Beef
ROAST

The oomph of flavour that comes with roast beef, together with all the trimmings and gravy, means it's time to roll out an unashamedly big wine with plenty of tannin, because its flavours will dissipate when drunk with food (if you go for a more wimpy wine, it will just get lost). If you want go classic then a claret (red Bordeaux) is a good place to start because they're typically rich in flavour and smooth with food. Left Bank Bordeaux means mostly Cabernet Sauvignon, so these will be richer in style; Right Bank Bordeaux means mostly Merlot, so they will be a bit more supple; but both banks of the river plant both varieties, so the wines are usually a blend of the two.

There are plenty of modern rich reds around to go with beef, and California makes some especially good ones. Cabernet Sauvignon from the regions of Napa and Sonoma are the swanky options – these make bold reds with plenty of black fruit and a fair amount of tannin, which is important for this dish. You could also try a red Zinfandel, which is meaty and rich with plenty of earthy structure. If you are having roast veal, a lighter red like a Chianti could work, or even a richly textured white wine, like a Pinot Gris from Alsace.

GRILLED

Malbec and beef is a quintessential match no matter how you're eating it, and beef in one of its purest forms – when grilled with little or no other ingredients – is especially good with a ripe and fruity Malbec. There are two places where Malbec takes centre stage and they make very different styles of wine, but such is this intrinsic affinity of beef and this grape that they both work like a charm. In Argentina, and in the Mendoza Valley especially, Malbecs have a sweet blackcurrant flavour, with dense spice and full tannins. They're delicious and concentrated wines, perfect with beef. The other is in Cahors in south-west France, where Malbecs have more of an earthy character, with handsome richness and bold flavours.

BARBECUED

The smoky edge to beef cooked on a barbecue ramps up the flavour a notch or two, which means you can go even bolder with the wine choice. For me, that often means a full-on spicy Syrah/Shiraz. The black-pepper character from this grape is usually picked up in the wine wherever it's made, and if you go classic – like one from the Rhône, there's a good chance it will have a smoked bacon character, too. If you go for a southern hemisphere classic, like Australian Shiraz, the spice is often accentuated by a lovely dry-spice aroma and flavour, a bit like the Middle Eastern dry-spice mixture *dukkah*. Either of these wines would work. South Africa now makes sensational Syrah/Shiraz, too, especially in Swartland, or you could try South African Pinotage, famous for its smoky flavour.

RAW & CURED

Steak tartare is great with bold reds that are very fruity and don't have too much tannin. Try a Côtes du Rhône.

STEWS & CASSEROLES

There are as many versions of beef stew as there are wines to go with it. That said, a rich red wine is needed, but not necessarily one that's as huge in tannin or as gutsy as what you'd drink with roast beef. Boeuf Bourguignon is made with Pinot Noir and is best when drunk with a smooth red Burgundy. Meanwhile, a slow-cooked beef stew with plenty of herbs would be terrific with a French red wine from further south in France. Try a Gigondas from the Rhône Valley, or a Grenache-Syrah-Mourvèdre blend from the Languedoc-Roussillon region in France, which tastes of herbs and is rich in black-fruit flavours.

PIES

The meaty filling and rich, buttery pastry calls for a wine that has a meatiness to match, but it's good to get a red that has a creamy dimension to it as well. To my mind, that means a smooth and rich red Rioja.

Lamb
ROAST

As with beef, the ultimate roast lamb needs the ultimate red wine, and luckily we're not short on choice. Something big and rich with real depth of flavour speaks to me of European classics like Brunello di Montalcino from Tuscany, especially if there are herbs involved. Brunello is a big and butch wine that's best when it's a bit older, so that the tannins have softened a little, but even then the wine is still quite meaty. Another option would be to go for a full-on Spanish red like a Priorat or a Ribera del Duero. Again, try not to drink them too young, as they mellow beautifully with age, and roast lamb is a dish that likes a mellow but rich wine.

GRILLED

The juiciness of a lamb kebab or grilled lamb chops is a sure bet with a firm and juicy wine that's been basking in the sunshine of the Mediterranean or New World. Agiorgitiko is a Greek grape that's bursting with sweet, plummy fruit and is best made in the region of the Peloponnese called Nemea. Seek out another great undiscovered red from the Croatian grape Plavac Mali. Or for something more familiar, try an energetic fruit-popping Shiraz or Cabernet Sauvignon from Australia.

BARBECUED

Time and again Chilean Syrah has been a winner for me with any kind of lamb on the barbecue. There's something about the black-pepper, savoury character and the purity and elegance of the blackberry fruit that sings really well with a touch of smokiness of the lamb. A richer choice is Chilean Carmenère, a robust and rich red.

STEWS

Earthy, deep and rich red wines are best with a lamb stew. A luscious red from Languedoc-Roussillon, or something from the New World, like a Bonarda. A Bonarda from Argentina is a good choice; its richness and spicy flavour would taste great. Or try a silky-smooth, minty Cabernet Sauvignon from Australia that has the power to stand up to this dish.

PIES

For dishes where the lamb has been minced, diced or chopped and there's a topping, a smooth – dare I say, lighter – red is a great choice. Cue Pinot Noir, one of the most versatile red grapes around. While it can be delicate, there are also some confident, richer Pinot Noirs cut there, so try one from Central Otago or Martinborough in New Zealand. If you're keen on staying in Europe, find an Etna Rosso from Sicily – it's deliciously smooth.

SALADS

If lamb is the lead flavour in a salad, and especially if there's beetroot/beet involved, go for a bottle of Pinot Noir. One of the great things about Pinot Noir (and of course, there are several) is its balance between succulent, soft fruit and earthiness, which is great with cold lamb.

Pork
ROAST

Having reared my own pigs in the past, I think I've tried every wine-and-pork flavour combination under the sun, and one of the things I discovered back then was that roast pork can go with red and white wine. A bright and fruity Pinot Noir is a safe bet, especially one with lovely plump fruit, like those from the Russian River Valley in California or Mornington Peninsula in Australia. One region that's worth checking out for both its white and red wines with roast pork is the Rhône Valley in France. Here, the whites are especially good at matching fruits (which are often served with pork) as well as for cutting through the crackling. They are dry wines made from grapes like Viognier, Marsanne and Roussanne (sometimes two or three of these together). That said, red from the Rhône can also work really well, but I'd pick something young and fruity, like a perky Côtes du Rhône-Villages.

RIBS

When ribs are sticky and slathered in gooey barbecue sauce, two styles of red spring to mind. Firstly, Syrah/Shiraz, because it has this ripe, jammy flavour and is delicious with the barbecue sauce. It doesn't just have to be Australian; any ripe New World style would be great. My Old World suggestion is a super-ripe red from Portugal, which is made from the same grapes that are used to make Port.

SAUSAGES & CASSEROLES

Herbs and other sausage ingredients can alter the wine choice here, but if you're talking a fairly basic recipe, whether it's sausages, stuffing or meatloaf, the same wines as I recommend for roast pork work brilliantly. Again, it's worth looking at the origins of these dishes; for example, with a serious sausage and lentil dish, the earthy, rich wines from Italy are mind-blowing, like a Super Tuscan, Barolo or Barbaresco; and for something a little less in-your-face, a Rosso di Montalcino. But then, if you're having a classic French cassoulet, there are some fantastic local reds around, like the hearty reds of Madiran and Cahors, and Marcillac for something a little lighter.

CURED

With so many variations on cured meat and ham according to country, I'm usually led by origin of the meat as a wine guide. A classic side of ham, though, is great with a juicy New World Pinot Noir, or a Beaujolais. Smoked ham, like bacon, is a no-brainer with the smoky, bacon-tasting reds from the Rhône. Spanish cured meats like chorizo, are great with a dry amontillado or fino Sherry. Yes, they are! If the pork is French, a juicy Beaujolais or a slightly chilled red from the Loire, made from Pinot Noir or Cabernet Franc, works brilliantly. Whereas Italian charcuterie like Parma ham is best with grapes that make light and fruity reds like Dolcetto or Frappato. As a general rule, a punchy, dry rosé made from Cabernet Sauvignon or Malbec, or those from Navarra in Spain, are good all-rounders with charcuterie.

Poultry
CHICKEN
Roast

The rich and comforting flavours of roast chicken are best with a wine that has those same qualities, so a supple, nutty, gently oaked Chardonnay is the out-and-out winner here. If you're in France, or just want to be in France, look at the richer and more expensive styles of Chablis: Premier Cru and Grand Cru. If you want a

white Burgundy, that can work, too – the expensive choice would be Puligny-Montrachet; the value-for-money choice would be Rully. In the southern hemisphere, Australia's Mornington Peninsula is crafting some seriously elegant Chardonnay that is a great choice with roast chicken. And speaking of Australia, if you really can't do Chardonnay, then pick up a bottle of slightly aged Semillon from the Hunter Valley instead – it's full of nutty, waxy flavour.

Smoked

A smoked chicken tastes more of smoke than chicken, so an oaked Chenin Blanc from South Africa is a lovely match to pick up on this smoky flavour.

Pie

Creamy chicken in a pastry coating is a winner with Chardonnay, again. Perhaps with the extra buttery richness you want a full and frank style, so try a Californian Chardonnay, one from Limari in Chile, or from Mendoza in Argentina.

Casserole

Chicken and red wine go hand-in-hand with casseroles and chicken pot dishes, because the red wine does a great job at bringing all the other ingredients together. For Coq au Vin, Pinot Noir is a no-brainer classic, and depending on how rich the sauce is, you could really push the boat out and try a full-on Syrah instead, which can also work with tomato-based sauces.

Garlic

When chicken and garlic come together, a white wine that has lots of texture (but isn't too aromatic) is best. Something like a French or South African Roussanne would be great.

ROAST GOOSE

This expensive, fatty meat is best matched with wines that happen to be pricey. I'd usually go for a Barolo with a few years of age on it. But that's assuming you're having a red wine. It might seem bizarre, but German Spätlese Riesling actually works brilliantly. It does a beautiful job at cutting through fatty meat, and is especially good with apple sauce.

ROAST DUCK

Although less pungent than goose, duck meat is rich and dark and I find it's best with bright red wines. I'd pick a Beaujolais from a robust Cru, like Moulin-à-Vent or a Pinot Noir from Marlborough in New Zealand or a Barbera from Piedmont. Serving confit duck? Or is fruit playing a major role in the dish? Try Pinot Gris or Pinot Blanc from Alsace.

Game
VENISON

Of all the game meats, venison is the one where you can really bring out the big wine guns. Grapes that make wines with an earthy, mushroom or truffle character are awesome, as they really heighten that umami game flavour, so try a truffle-laden wine made with Nebbiolo, like a Barolo or Barbaresco. If the budget doesn't stretch to this, try a Langhe Nebbiolo instead. Pure fruit is great for the density of lean venison, especially when served as carpaccio or with beetroot/beets. Venison is the meat that's commonly paired with rich sauces like chocolate or balsamic vinegar. Even though these aren't very wine-friendly, it's worth going for a big southern Rhône red like a Châteauneuf-du-Pape, or even something with a hint of sweetness, like an Amarone della Valpolicella.

wild boar

The depth of flavour of wild boar makes it a low-maintenance match with red wines, provided the tannin is kept to a minimum. Grape varieties native to Italy are fantastic. Try a Barbera from Piedmont, or a Sangiovese from Tuscany, like a Chianti that isn't too oaky. If wild boar is served as charcuterie, try a slightly chilled Beaujolais.

RABBIT & HARE

The wine choice for these depends on what they're cooked with. If there's cream or white wine involved, go for dry Pinot Gris, Pinot Blanc or a dry-ish Vouvray, which is made from Chenin Blanc. But if it's cooked in red wine, then a rustic red works brilliantly with the gamey flavours. Try a Marcillac from south-west France, or an Aglianico from Campania.

PIGEON

Pigeon needs a big and bold black-fruited wine to do it justice, and something with lots of grip to the tannin. Try Bandol in southern France, Aglianico from Italy, claret, or Priorat from Spain.

PARTRIDGE, PHEASANT & QUAIL

Never a letdown with these birds, Pinot Noir is a hard-to-beat pairing. It has both earthiness and delicacy, we just need to be on tannin-watch here, because unlike pigeon, these meats will struggle to cope with very strong tannins. Sometimes these meats are served with a white sauce and if this is the case, a white that doesn't shout too loudly is best, making Chardonnay the perfect choice.

GUINEA FOWL

I've had success with a variety of wines and guinea fowl in the past, but Burgundy's main grapes, Pinot Noir and Chardonnay, are both hard to beat. A prettier Pinot Noir like Volnay will bring out the gamey flavour of this white meat, while the Chardonnay with a touch of oak like Saint Véran also plays to guinea fowl's sensibilities. Aged Semillon from the Hunter Valley in Australia is my wildcard option.

Pâté & terrine

Plenty of wines go with pâtés or terrines, because they have many ingredients. In France, Beaujolais is the classic catch-all pork terrine match, but any other light red would work, like red Sancerre or Austrian Zweigelt. Foie Gras, controversial though it is, is enhanced by both toasty sparkling wines like Champagne and sweet wines like Sauternes. Pacherenc du Vic-Bilh is a real winner. And if you're up for Sherry, a dry amontillado has a tangy freshness that's very duck terrine-friendly. It's decadent, but when it comes to fatty pork rillettes, nothing beats a frisky glass of Champagne or Crémant.

Offal
HAGGIS

This famous Scottish delicacy is essentially an offal sausage, and it's traditionally served with swedes and mashed potatoes. Being Scottish and rich in flavour, you can see why whisky is regarded as a 'classic' match, but haggis is also great with a red wine, and really there are plenty of choices, although my ideal would be a rich and serious Beaujolais, or even with a Pouilly-Fuissé, a Chardonnay with guts.

FAGGOTS

Usually served with gravy, this mixture of various offal cuts has a soft texture and very meaty flavour. It's great with a wine where Tempranillo is the main grape, but would also work with those GSM blends.

OXTAIL & BEEF CHEEK

The tail and cheek are usually rich and gelatinous, so full-bodied reds are good here. Try Malbec from Argentina or Cahors, Tannat from Madiran or Uruguay, Brunello di Montalcino or Californian Zinfandel.

LIVER & KIDNEY

Although red wine is an obvious choice here, the best ones for liver and kidney are low in tannin and acid, which are two elements to a wine that can make the offal taste aggressive, almost steely, in the mouth. This calls for either something plump from the Rhône, or in Spain, a Garnacha would be lovely.

PIG'S HEAD & TROTTERS

Although these quite can be quite gelatinous in texture once they've been cooked, they're packed with flavour. Try a Rosso di Montalcino.

BLACK PUDDING

This is likely to be served to pep up a fish dish or as part of a fry-up. A firm and fruity Syrah/Shiraz is great with black pudding. If it's being served with, say scallops, then don't go so full-on – have a gutsy rosé instead.

Surf 'n' turf

Forget asparagus, artichoke or tomato – the ingredients that get a bad rap for being difficult to drink with wine. The ultimate wine challenge is to find one that works with two completely different ingredients on one plate. This is surf 'n' turf's dilemma in a nutshell. To solve this potential dining headache I've picked out wine choices for two completely different versions of surf 'n' turf, because food now transcends so many cultures that there are a million ways to interpret it.

Classic surf 'n' turf: steak & lobster

Assume here that the fruity meat of a lobster is slathered with butter while the steak is medium-rare.

PREMIER CRU OR GRAND CRU CHABLIS, AT LEAST 8 YEARS OLD

In my mind, this is about the only white wine that really has the guts and wherewithal to be able to stand up to steak. These two levels of Chablis are the most expensive ones, and because the Chardonnay fruit in them is such high quality, they have enough character to put up with extra richness from ageing in oak barrels. Contact with the barrel gives them a nutty, malty, buttery flavour which is great with the rich and buttery lobster meat. However, there is often also a bacon-fat richness of flavour, which gives it enough 'meatiness' for the steak. If you go for a Premier Cru, make it a robust one, like Montée de Tonnerre or Fourchaume.

VINTAGE ROSÉ CHAMPAGNE, AT LEAST 10 YEARS OLD

Champagne is a fantastically food-friendly wine; that's a given. Rosé Champagne, which usually has a portion of red wine blended into it to give it the pink colour, has the perfect red-fruit flavour for fruity lobster meat. Rosé Champagne is more robust than white Champagne, and when rosé Champagne ages it takes on a rich, meaty flavour that can also cope with the richness of a steak.

Upside-down surf 'n' turf: cod & pancetta

This popular restaurant dish could also work with the classic surf 'n' turf wines, even though they don't need to be quite so old and rich. However, a much more successful pairing is red wine.

'So, why not the red wine with the steak?' I hear you ask. Well, both the cod and ham can stand up to a red wine, but this kind of red wine that's lighter, would get lost with a beefy steak.

PINOT NOIR

Being a versatile little grape, it doesn't matter too much where the Pinot Noir comes from, because it inherently has a lightness of touch to it as a red wine. This means it can work with fish, and especially 'meaty' fish like cod, but because it's a red wine it also has enough fleshy flavours, and sometimes a hint of smoke, too, to stand up to the pancetta. My choice would be one from Oregon in America or Central Otago in New Zealand.

fish & shellfish

One of the most common wine myths in the world applies to this chapter – that red wine and fish don't work – but it's untrue. You can see exactly how and why below, but really, it's just about common sense, because something crazy like pairing oysters with a blockbuster Australian Shiraz is never going to work, is it? Wacky pairings aside, there are so many species of fish, not to mention ways in which they can be cooked, it only stands to reason that fish can be paired with all sorts of wine styles, from sparkling to still, white to red and even light to fortified wine. That said, you'll probably see common wines featured through these pages. Perky, floral, zesty whites are mentioned a lot, especially those from coastal regions, plus there is always a case for marrying local wine with local food. In coastal areas, for example, the wine and food both carry a salty streak through their flavours, inherently making them a fantastic match.

Raw, marinated & salted

CEVICHE

Sauvignon Blanc or Torrontés

With zingy and vibrant South American-inspired marinated fish like ceviche, you want a wine in the same league. A classic match in this respect, and one that's always been a winner for me, has been a Sauvignon Blanc that's zesty, grapefruit-sour and über-fresh, like unoaked Sauvignon Blanc from New Zealand, Chile or South Africa. But if you wanted to go a bit more 'local', try Torrontés, which is Argentina's flagship white grape. It's eye-poppingly fresh and has an intense, baby-powder aroma, but don't let that put you off! It's supremely juicy and fresh in the mouth, making it a winner with the zip and zing of ceviche.

SUSHI & SASHIMI

Chablis & delicate Old World whites

The cleansing and fresh flavour of fish that shines through in sushi and especially sashimi, usually calls for something that's light enough not to overpower the delicacy of the fish, but that has enough drive to enhance the fish flavour (and, by the way, I'd recommend going easy on the soy sauce and wasabi if you really want the fish and wine to show at their best together). There are many fish-friendly wines; most are crisp and cleansing whites. An easy-to-find,

fail-safe choice would be Chablis. As in a youthful Chablis, not its superiors, Premier Cru or Grand Cru Chablis – because these two are likely to have oak influence. When it's good, this can be one of the purest-tasting wines in the world.

Old World whites

Want something a bit less classic than Chablis? There are loads of other choices, even in Europe. What about Portugal? Vinho Verde is really fresh and pretty, especially those from the Loureiro grape; or what about a white Douro (yes, the place that's also the home of Port)? The Douro Valley now makes sensationally crisp whites from local grape varieties.

GRAVLAX

Grüner Veltliner

Even thinking about this pairing is whetting my appetite. The fresh, green flavours of dill paired with the smokiness of salmon, and quite possibly, a touch of horseradish also thrown into the mix, all these are singing out for a glass of Grüner Veltliner. It's Austria's leading white wine grape, and a sommelier's favourite for its versatility. Grüner Veltliner is citrus-fresh and herbaceous, but its hallmark is the white-pepper spice that really gives it extra personality and perkiness.

Crustaceans

LOBSTER

Champagne

If you're splashing out on something like lobster thermidor, you might as well go the whole hog and drink it with Champagne, don't you think? After all, the two are such a brilliant match, because Champagne has a good balance of toasty richness – to match the lobster's concentrated flavour – as well as a freshness to lighten it. This makes a Blanc de Blancs Champagne the ultimate match with lobster, because it's the style of Champagne best known for this rich-but-fresh balance.

PRAWNS, SHRIMPS & LANGOUSTINES

Spanish whites

As varied as the choice of prawn/shrimp dishes can be, in my experience there isn't much that a decent Albariño can't pair brilliantly. Albariño is Spain's most famous white wine, of course, and it comes from the north-west coast, Rías Baixas. It's a match made in heaven with seafood, especially because of its fresh, salty lick from the sea air freshening up the ripe fruit.

Then there's Godello. This up-and-coming Spanish white grape makes richer, more peachy-flavoured whites than Albariño, so I'd choose it with prawn/

Molluscs

There's a reason why oysters and Champagne are a quintessential match. It's delicious! Clams, scallops and winkles all love being served with a zesty Sauvignon Blanc or a lighter Chablis.

shrimp flavours with a bit more oomph, maybe with a dash of spice or garlic. And if you're feeling brave, serve richer prawns/shrimps with a floral, zesty fino or manzanilla Sherry.

CRAB

Sauvignon Blanc or rosé

Dressed crab, crab salad, crab cakes; it doesn't matter what the dish, one of these two wines usually comes up a treat with crab. The best Sauvignon Blancs for this food are unoaked and mineral-driven, which typically means they're from a cooler climate. The classics from the Loire, Sancerre and Pouilly-Fumé, are the perfect fit, or if you want something delicious but less of a talking point, hunt down a Sauvignon Blanc from a region in the north-east of Italy, like Friuli.

If you go for rosé, these should also be delicate and dry (unless you're having Thai crab cakes because the spice would like a slightly sweeter rosé, like one from California, perhaps). France is also a good place in this respect: a Cabernet Franc rosé from the Loire, or one from Provence. Want something a bit unusual? Try a rosé Vinho Verde – they make light and pretty pink wines as well as light whites.

Pink fish

Rosé & light reds

The sweetness of meat as well as the richer texture in salmon, trout and tuna make them natural partners with pink or light-red wines. Even though I say 'red', I'm talking about reds that are on the lighter, fresher end of the spectrum, and definitely not ones that are heavy in body, alcohol or tannin. This means reds from cooler climates or red grapes that are naturally lighter in weight. A combination of the two would be perfect, such as a classic Beaujolais, which is made from the

For best results with these light reds, I'd whack the bottle in the fridge for 10-25 minutes before serving. See page 31 for more on chilling red wine.

Gamay grape and is full of perky raspberry fruit. Dishes with not so many ingredients can take a lighter Pinot Noir, whether it's from England or France.

For pink-fleshed fish with more attitude, you can ramp up a Pinot Noir gear and look at those from Oregon, New Zealand or Chile. Or if you want a different grape altogether, try an Etna Rosso from Sicily, or a light Mencía from Bierzo in Spain.

Rosés are great, too. As I said for the shellfish, I'd go for dry ones. And although Provençal rosé and tuna Niçoise are *the* perfect match (a classic example of matching food and wine from the same region), in general, I'd say pink-fleshed fish can take a rosé that's a bit bigger in personality than white-fleshed fish. Have a look at Spain; the rosés from Navarra, often made with Garnacha, are pretty buxom and juicy. Or Portugal, which is also making punchy rosés from native grapes like Touriga Nacional. Puglia in southern Italy makes fantastic rosés for fish from the Negroamaro grape.

Baked & grilled white fish
Italian whites
In my mind, easy-to-make meals should mean easy-to-drink wines. And with so many different options of what to add to the flavour of baked or grilled fish, I usually turn to a country that's very versatile. There's one winner when it comes to this: Italy, which is one of the best and most exciting places to find food-friendly, fresh-as-a-daisy whites, but also whites with extra richness and texture, should you need that for a white fish dish that's crammed with different flavours.

I'm not just talking about the grape Pinot Grigio or the style Soave (which is made from a grape called Garganega), either. I'm talking about diving into the melting pot of tangy, lesser-known white grapes and styles, because Italy has tonnes of them. For example, far up in the north-east where Italy borders Slovenia, the region of Friuli serves up lovely fresh whites from the floral Friulano and zesty Malvasia; while in Tuscany and Sardinia, the lemon-and-spice-flavoured main white grape there is Vermentino (known as Rolle in the south of France). Down in the south, Fiano is a well-known match for fish, but Grillo also has a lemony freshness and is worth checking out. All of these are great with freshly grilled white fish and a simple squeeze of fresh lemon.

For white fish married with lots of flavour, whether it's influenced by herbs, a rich-based sauce or with a bit of spice, richer Italian whites are good. In the north that could mean Chardonnay from Lombardy called Curtefranca; a nutty-flavoured grape from Friuli, called Ribolla Gialla; Verdicchio dei Castelli di Jesi from Marche, or a good Greco di Tufo from Campania.

Smoked
Chardonnay
There's one grape variety I've consistently found to be great with smoked fish: Chardonnay. Not massive, oaky Chardonnays; nor very light, unoaked ones, but somewhere between the two. A Chardonnay with subtle oak blends beautifully with the smokiness of a fish like smoked salmon, and I've had more than a few melting moments of smoked haddock fishcakes with a glass of Chardonnay, too. Where to find them? Have a peek at those from New Zealand – most regions make it consistently well. Limarí is a relatively new region in Chile but its Chardonnays are looking delicious. Check out Burgundy and Argentina, too, by all means, but as a general rule, the more expensive the Chardonnay, the greater chance it will have more oak.

Chenin Blanc & Chenin Blanc blends
The ABC (anything but Chardonnay) crowd should try a Chenin Blanc from South Africa. These wines mirror Chardonnay's ability to soak up oak flavours, but the flavour tastes less of apples and butter than Chardonnays with oak. There are some incredible lightly smoky Chenin Blanc wines being made here these days, both in the classic area of Stellenbosch and the up-and-coming region Swartland (which is making some really exciting wines that the wine industry refer to as 'white blends'). This just means they're from a mixture of grapes, but usually Chenin Blanc, which is the signature South African white grape, makes up the base of these wines, and I can't stress enough how much these are wines to watch out for. They are great with fish that have been whipped straight off the barbecue with their smoky, charred flavour.

Oily
Dry rosé
Mackerel and sardines speak of the summer, and are at their best when freshly caught and thrown straight on the grill. Oily fish need crisp wines to cut through the oiliness, and for this, it's hard to beat a rosé. Rosé also speaks of the summer, so the two really are a great match, whether the mackerel has been paired with some tangy citrus fruit in a salad or the sardine has a splash of chilli on it. Portuguese and Spanish rosés really tick the box here, but don't forget France's nerve centre of rosé, Provence. You don't have to be limited to just those locations, though. The sunshine in California and Australia makes some great rosés from all sorts of varieties, and the same applies to Chile. Just try to keep it dry.

Fried
Fizz
From soft-shell crab to fish and chips, the serious wine-matching component in these dishes is actually

the batter, which needs something to cut through the fat covering the seafood. Cue sparkling wine. Champagne with fish and chips is one of my all-time favourite food and wine combinations. There's something decadent about partnering a meal that's wrapped in newspaper with one of the most prestigious wine styles in the world. It feels wrong but also right (actually, it's only ever felt right to me). Anyway, the combination of rich fruit, bubbles and fresh acidity make this a seamless match, especially if the fizz is made from pure Chardonnay. Having said that, although Champagne has been my go-to wine for fish and chips for years, I've increasingly been drinking it with English sparkling wine. Call me biased, but these wines are now excellent in quality and have extra freshness to them (what with England being cooler than Champagne) and that makes them a perfect match. Plus, of course, it adheres to that notion of matching local food and wine – Britain's favourite Friday-night takeout with its very best fizz.

Light & frisky whites

If bubbles don't work for you, then a frisky, fresh white that comes straight from the coast is perfect. The Muscadet grape makes a delicate, pretty wine, just off the west coast of northern France. Greece's Assyrtiko grape is as refreshing as it is floral. Or if you want to track something down that's a bit more unusual, try a Croatian grape called Pošip *(say it: posh-ip)*, which makes delicious, zesty white wines on a little island on the Dalmatian Coast called Korčula. Pošip is crisp, with hardcore sour fruit and a salty tang. It's lovely stuff, and worth tracking down.

Seafood pasta

When it comes to pasta, it's usually the sauce that takes the flavour in different directions, and seafood pasta is no different. I have a few tips for this, and they're easily broken down by whether a wine is Italian or not, following that local-pairing thinking once more.

Italian
For a classic Italian wine match, try *rosato* from any of Italy's winemaking regions. Or for extra indulgence, what about a fizzy, rosé Franciacorta? The white grapes Grillo and Falanghina would also be delicious with seafood pasta dishes like spaghetti puttanesca or spaghetti vongole.

Non-Italian
For non-Italian wine try both Old and New World rosés or unoaked Chardonnays.

Time-saver tip: go pink
If you're really short on time to track down a specific seafood match, a bold, dry rosé is a pretty safe bet, even ones that have a kick of chilli or some pungent herbs added to the dish.

veg

Whether as the main event, or in a supporting role, vegetables can be just as much of a game-changer when it comes to matching wines as spice or sauce can be. This section is about more than just vegetables, though; it also delves into the foods that are often served alongside them, such as eggs, lentils and pulses.

Salads

PANZANELLA

One of my all-time favourites, this salad with humble leftover origins is mostly made up of tomatoes and bread together with herbs, onions and a bit of basil, as well as a very generous glug of olive oil. Given it's from Tuscany, it seems crazy to go for a wine from anywhere else, and, in fact, many Tuscan wines work well. Try a fresh, bouncy and youthful Sangiovese with sappy, raspberry-flavoured fruit to pair with the tomatoes, or try one of those lovely herbal-flavoured Tuscan *rosatos*. And if you want white, the Tuscan white Vermentino grape is zesty, herbaceous and fresh.

TRICOLORE

Avocado, tomato and mozzarella make a holistic and delicious combination, but when it comes to wine it's not an easy thing to match. Go for a tropical New Zealand Sauvignon Blanc or an Italian Verdicchio.

GREEK

Keeping it local (and therefore simple) seems like the obvious thing to do here. With the chalky feta cheese and crisp, summery flavours, the perky Greek Assyrtiko grape is a winner, although it's not always easy to come by, so you can substitute it with a crisp Sauvignon Blanc.

NIÇOISE

Whether there's tuna in this or not, the home of the Niçoise salad in the south of France is also home to its ultimate pairing – a fruity, dry rosé from Provence.

CAESAR

Although we may think of it in 'salad' terms as light in flavour, the components of this salad are actually pretty rich: Parmesan cheese, garlic in the dressing, and even more so if you add anchovies and chicken. The best match for all these punchy flavours is Grüner Veltliner, which, despite being zippy and zingy, also has enough power behind it to stand up to the Caesar ingredients. If you wanted to stay French, go for a Chablis otherwise a Chardonnay with a bit of attitude – it'll work as long as it isn't too buttery or oaky.

BEETROOT/BEET & GOAT'S CHEESE

The yin and yang of these ingredients is why they work so well together but it's also why they're not the easiest to match with wine. However, although the beetroot/beet has plenty of flavour in its own right, the dense flavour and chalky texture of the goat's cheese is the dominant component here, and it leads us straight to Sauvignon Blanc, which has an unparalleled affinity with goat's cheese.

SALADS WITH FRUIT

Waldorf salad is creamy and has both apples and nuts to match with wine. The sweetness of fruit and floral character in English Bacchus is a delicious pairing, or the ripe fruit of a dry-ish Pinot Gris from Alsace would also work. Floral Torrontés from Argentina is great, too.

Pear, chicory/endive and blue cheese salads usually need a slightly sweeter wine, not just to match the sweetness of the pear but also to cut through the blue cheese, which is the most pungent component in the

dish. Given a free choice, I'd go for an off-dry Vouvray, made from Chenin Blanc.

Halloumi, watermelon and green bean salad is all about dry rosé. This will counter the salty cheese and make the most of the crunchy watermelon. Although it should be dry in style, it should be packed with flavour, too, so a ripe rosé from New Zealand, Chile or Navarra is ideal.

Greens

Peas, beans, courgettes/zucchini, asparagus and so on, the nostril-tingling freshness of fresh green vegetables doesn't disappoint in the mouth and can be matched very easily with wines that mimic those herbaceous and green flavours. This is Sauvignon Blanc territory. In cooler climates like France, places like Sancerre, the grassy flavour is light and delicate, but if there's significant richness to the dish, like in a creamy risotto primavera for example, then a fuller Sauvignon Blanc, like those from Chile, New Zealand or South Africa, is better.

Artichoke

This can be a tricky one, because wine often brings out the sourness and bitterness in artichokes, which means most reds (because of the tannins) are a no-no. If you're into Sherry it's good news, because the dry fino or manzanilla styles, which are like a zesty white wine, can be delicious. But if Sherry isn't for you, a richer white like some of the more nutty, waxy ones from Italy can work. A Falanghina, Verdicchio or a Ribolla Gialla are brilliant options. For all that, one of my biggest artichoke-and-wine successes has been with a dry Australian Riesling from Clare Valley, whose zingy, lime character really opened out with artichoke.

Fennel

Famous for its aniseed flavour, fennel can be served in a variety of ways, from shredded and raw in a salad to braised and stuffed. The longer it's cooked, the fainter the aniseed pungency. So, if the fennel is at maximum flavour when served raw, it's best with a herbal white wine like Sauvignon Blanc, Albariño, Vermentino, or Grüner Veltliner. If the fennel is cooked but not covered in a sauce of any kind, try a German Riesling, which should pick up on the aniseed flavour but remain juicy and fresh – a Kabinett could work but I'd sooner have a Spätlese.

Tomatoes
RAW

This 'wine and tomatoes don't work' business is a mystery to me; I've never really found it to be a problem. The go-to grape (as it often seems to be in this veg section!) is Sauvignon Blanc. Even though this is a very crisp wine, as are (acidic) raw tomatoes, the grassy freshness of Sauvignon Blanc always makes the most of the pungent vine flavour with a naked tomato. In recipes like tomato salsa or gazpacho, which have a tangy bite to the tomato flavour, the classic match is actually Sherry, the light and dry fino or manzanilla. It's a dream pairing, really.

COOKED

A different beast altogether to the raw version. When tomatoes are squidgy and plump they taste fleshy rather than fruity. This means the wine match changes significantly, because now we're in red wine territory. Nothing too big, and especially nothing too tannic. Try a smooth Côtes du Rhône-Villages with something like ratatouille – the herbs in the dish will be picked up by this style of wine – or try an unoaked New World Pinot Noir. If there's buttery pastry involved, like with a tomato tart, you could go back to a richer white that matches the pastry, so a slightly oaky Chardonnay or even a lightly oaked Sauvignon Blanc – often called Fumé Blanc in California – would be fantastic.

Mushrooms & truffles

The heavenly, woody, earthy pungency of mushrooms and truffles can provide the opportunity for some off-the-charts successful wine pairings. Naturally, it's the inherently earthy wines that work best.

In white wine terms, we're talking about Chardonnay. When Chardonnay has a bit of oak to it, the earthy flavour is accentuated, so this would be the choice for something simple like a mushroom terrine on toast.

There are more options with red wine. Most of them centre around the earthy, mineral-led Pinot Noir, which to me comes from Burgundy, Germany, Alsace and northern Italy. Blaufränkisch from Austria is an unorthodox – but also great – choice.

To match the hedonistic earthiness of mushroom and truffle, the answer lies in Piedmont. Here, the grapes Barbera and especially Nebbiolo are deliciously earthy and pungent. To really push the boat out, an older, relaxed Nebbiolo from Barolo or Barbaresco make a heavenly match with everything from mushroom risotto to scrambled eggs with shaved truffle on top.

PASTA

As with seafood (see page 145), when mushrooms or truffles are used in pasta sauce, we have to think of the flavours differently. Here are my picks for Italian and non-Italian red and white wines that work well with a variety of mushroom-flavoured pasta dishes.

Italian red
Pinot Nero, Nebbiolo (including Barolo and Barbaresco), Etna Rosso, Rosso di Montalcino, Sagrantino

Italian white
Aged Franciacorta

Non-Italian red
Pinot Noir

Non-Italian white
A richer, slightly oaked Chardonnay

Winter vegetables

Beetroot/beets, parsnip and carrot usually require something mellow to work with due to the sweetness in these vegetables that comes out when they're

Vegetable cakes

With carrot cake, try a Tawny Port. Not only is there sweetness from the carrot to consider, but there's spice from the cinnamon and nutmeg, earthiness from the walnuts and citrus from the orange, all perfect for a Tawny. For beetroot/beet cake, match the rich, earthy sweetness of beetroot/beet with Banyuls, a sweet red wine from the south of France. Or, if you want a dry wine, try a super-fruity Australian Shiraz, which sounds a bit crazy but it's definitely worth trying with the sweetness of beetroot/beet.

roasted or have been buttered. The same applies to pumpkin and butternut squash, which are fruity but slightly earthy. Try southern French-inspired white grapes like Viognier, Roussanne and Marsanne, which are not only found in France but in Australia, South Africa and California these days. Cabernet Sauvignon is also known to be a good match for carrot.

Potatoes

Being more of a flavour-absorber than having lots of natural flavour, there's no catch-all wine match with potatoes because it depends on how they're cooked and what other flavours are thrown at them. Fried potatoes and those slathered in butter are best with a crisp Chardonnay or a sparkling wine that cuts through the fat, but for everything else, it depends on the other ingredients in a dish.

Onion & garlic
GARLIC & RAW ONION

When the pungency of garlic or the sharp tang of raw onion is the key ingredient, a dry, crisp, tangy wine is best. Try a juicy but grapefruit-sour Sauvignon Blanc from Casablanca in Chile, which is great with everything from garlic bread to salsa verde.

COOKED ONION

Cooking onions brings out an intense flavour and sweetness, especially when caramelized in dishes like French onion soup or onion tart. You could go with a red wine here like Beaujolais, but I'm far more tempted by a smooth and buttery French Chardonnay.

Eggs
OMELETTE, PANCAKES & FRITTATA

Dressing eggs up lightly with a sprinkle of herbs or cheese usually lends itself well to a wine that's fresh

but with some oomph of flavour: a New Zealand Chardonnay or a mineral-fresh Chablis. If the eggs are jazzed up with richer flavours like ham, mushrooms, tomatoes, red (bell) peppers or spice, then a Beaujolais or other juicy red wine is great. If there are a lot of green herbs, a slightly chilled Cabernet Franc from the Loire is a nice crunchy option that's herbal in flavour to match, or English Pinot Noir works, too.

BRUNCH EGGS

Call me decadent, but there's not much that a good sparkling wine can't sort out with scrambled eggs, fried eggs or even poached eggs on a muffin with sauce draped over the top. Champagne has the acidity to cut through the yolk of the egg and richness of a sauce like hollandaise, so any white and traditional fermentation sparkling wine could work (see pages 126–129).

Fried food

Frying is such a powerful game-changer for wine matching, because the oily, rich nature of the food usually overrides the flavour of the ingredients. This applies to meat and fish, too, of course, but as for vegetables, whether it's a delicate courgette/zucchini flower, vegetable burger, herbal arancini or the humble potato fries, the key to wine matching is all in the freshness. By freshness I mean crisp acidity, so firstly look for that, and secondly (but only if you want to go one step further), let yourself be guided by region. Freshness is accentuated by bubbles so sparkling wine always works well with fried food. Using the examples above, pair arancini with Franciacorta, fries with English sparkling wine or Champagne, and courgette/zucchini flower with a Crémant de Loire or again, a Champagne.

Rice, pulses & grains

LENTILS & RICE

Although lentils have a creamy, earthy flavour to them, it's often other flavours that lead the dish. A hearty lentil and vegetable soup is usually a winner with a comforting, smooth red from the south of France, or a Beaujolais that isn't served too cold. Because rice absorbs flavour, its wine choices are all about the flavours it soaks up. For a risotto primavera with greens and Parmesan, a Pinot Grigio, Soave or Sauvignon Blanc work best, while a butternut squash/pumpkin risotto is lovely with a ripe and peachy-flavoured wine like Godello from Spain or a Viognier from France. Mushroom risotto is classically paired with earthy Barbera from Piedmont or a Burgundian Pinot Noir.

CORN

With the sweet kernels of corn, whether in a chowder or salad, young and zesty New World Semillon is most definitely the answer. The plump juiciness of a fresh New Zealand or Australian Semillon would work just perfectly.

CHICKPEAS

The chalky texture of chickpeas is probably more important than its flavour, which isn't really that powerful on its own. Once it's made with other ingredients, though, like in falafel, a crisp and fresh, herbal-flavoured wine works best, so try a dry and zingy Australian Riesling, or a dry Loureiro.

COUSCOUS

When couscous is served up with a tomato-based vegetable sauce, see if you can find a ballsy Moroccan Carignan; if not, a Nero d'Avola from Sicily or a Negroamaro from Puglia. In a salad with orange, dried fruit and nuts, couscous is great with a dry Palo Cortado Sherry, which tastes of oranges, nuts, sultanas/golden raisins and apricots, so it's definitely the one to go for. Be bold!

sauce

Sauces have the potential to be game-changers when it comes to pairing food with wine, and when this happens, the wine should match the sauce, not whatever protein or carbohydrate is taking up most of the room on your plate or in your bowl.

Salsa verde

Salsa Verde's tongue-popping blend of herbs, garlic, lemon, anchovies, capers and olive oil – when paired with fish – cries out for Sauvignon Blanc. A South African Sauvignon Blanc would be delicious here, or if you want to try something a bit more quirky, try Spain – yes Spain. Rueda in north-west Spain is famous for its local grape Verdejo but it's now making some good Sauvignon Blanc, too. If the rest of the dish is also rich in flavour, try an oaked Sauvignon Blanc. Bordeaux and California (where it's often called Fumé Blanc) are the most famous regions for this style, but they're by no means exclusive in making it; quite a few New Zealand producers now make a very good version. A bit of oak on Sauvignon dumbs down its punchy fruit – although it's still crunchy and fresh in the mouth – but the oak peps up its texture, and because of this it's a style I only ever drink with food. When salsa verde is matched with red meat, it's best to drink a red that is known for having a herbal edge, to pick up on the herbs in the salsa. Wines with a good proportion of Cabernet Sauvignon or Cabernet Franc can be good here, because they both have classic herbal characters.

Onion gravy

Gravy implies a dish that's going to be rich and hearty, so you want a no-nonsense red, one that's rich and full of flavour. There's plenty of choice in this respect, but I'd go for a Tempranillo or GSM. The best wines made from Tempranillo (one of the main grapes in red Rioja) have a meaty, melt-in-your-mouth quality. They are full-bodied but mellow texture, especially if you have one that's at least three to four years old so it's had time to soften and relax. GSM refers to the three-grape blend of Grenache, Syrah/Shiraz and Mourvèdre, one of the most classic blended styles around. It's big, with lots of fruit and usually a lick of spice, too. This style's rich, sweet fruit is usually a perfect foil for the sweetness of onions in gravy. If you want to go classic, head to its home, France, where it's best from the southern Rhône Valley or Languedoc-Roussillon regions. That said, GSM is also popular in Australia (where Mourvèdre is sometimes called Mataro).

Hollandaise

Chablis is a great catch-all choice, and I say catch-all because hollandaise can be paired with any number of dishes – asparagus, artichoke, fish or eggs, so we need something crisp to cut through its creamy texture, but rich enough to stand up to its buttery flavour. We're talking Chardonnay that's rich or lightly oaked, and in Chablis, this usually means the higher end of the quality scale; a Premier Cru or Grand Cru. A Premier Cru is cheaper, and broadly speaking its oakiness is less overt, so I would probably go for that, or just a straight Chablis, which will have plenty of flavour even though it might be unoaked. A good-quality, lightly oaked Chardonnay from anywhere, as long as it's fresh and crisp, would do well. If you don't want Chardonnay, try the delicious, slightly apricot-flavoured grape Arneis from Piedmont in north-west Italy. This is sublime with hollandaise over eggs, while Albariño from north-west Spain is delicious with asparagus and hollandaise, Chardonnay too.

Tomato

Pairing wine with food from roughly the same place is a useful tip for any kind of wine-and-food matching, and nowhere is this better illustrated than with a tomato sauce-based dish, because it plays a major role in Italian food, and many of Italy's reds work with it. Because of the acidity in tomatoes, we want a red that's very juicy but not too heavy in tannin.

A smooth and supple Chianti would be sublime, but there's plenty to be had across the rest of Italy. In the north, Piedmont, the fruity Dolcetto gives you sweet fruit with plenty of freshness. There are a couple of fruity choices that I especially like from further south. One is red Lambrusco (seriously), which can be a little bit sparkling, and is incredible with pizza, too, while another easy-to-drink fruity red comes from the Frappato grape, which is light in colour and low in tannin.

Chocolate sauce

Matching chocolate with wine is notoriously tricky, but it's also one of our favourite dessert choices, especially when there are so many types of chocolate, and all those gooey fillings. If we're talking dark/ bittersweet chocolate, then red wine is the way to go – try a Brachetto d'Aqui, an Italian, light sparkling red. If we're not, a sweet wine like red Port might work, with a general rule that the richer the chocolate, the more serious the Port. But dry reds can work well too. I've had a few fantastic Australian Shiraz and chocolate pairings.

Horseradish

The beauty of horseradish – a bit like with salsa verde – is that its fiery punch can go with fish and meat. Either way, the heat demands a wine with attitude. If you're having fish, a fruity and aromatic wine from the coast is one option. This could mean Albariño, or just across the border from where this is made, in Portugal, the best Alvarinho (the same grape) is also delicious in Vinho Verde. Or, if you like New Zealand wines, go for a lovely bright Riesling from the region of Waipara. A quirkier, and delicious, alternative is Kerner. This is a super-aromatic grape that can be luscious, too, (although it usually makes a dry wine) and is made in Austria, Germany and Switzerland, although my personal favourite comes from Alto Adige in Italy.

Pasta sauces
MEAT & TOMATO

With dishes like lasagna and spaghetti bolognese, the trick is to respect the fruit needed for the tomato sauce while having something beefy enough for the weight of flavour you get with the meat. I'd go all-out Italian for these sauces: Montepulciano d'Abruzzo, Barbera, Chianti (made from Sangiovese) or Etna Rosso. If you'd rather go non-Italian try Pinot Noir, Syrah/Shiraz, Zweigelt or Beaujolais.

GREEN PESTO

Basil usually dominates the flavour here, making a perky white with a herbal or grassy flavour – one that has enough guts to match the Parmesan and pine nuts/kernels – the best choice. In Italy, go with Garganega (Soave), Verdicchio, Vermentino, Falanghina or Friulano. Everywhere else, try Sauvignon Blanc or Grüner Veltliner; and if you want red, Cabernet Franc or Merlot.

Store-cupboard wine matches

Those magic little pots and jars in your cupboards and fridges, which are usually packed with flavour and can change the taste of a dish altogether, depending on how much you add, can be tricky to pair with wine, so here are a few ideas to get you started.

Mustard
AUSTRALIAN SEMILLON
The heat and sharp tang of mustard works well with a mellow and slightly nutty wine like Australian Semillon.

Piccalilli
PINOT GRIGIO
Although the bite of the Indian spice and the types of vegetables can vary in this and other chutneys, a fruity Pinot Grigio copes really well, and especially if it's from the southern hemisphere, like New Zealand, where it's often really ripe and full.

Soy sauce
AMARONE DELLA VALPOLICELLA
Balance out the salty soy flavour with a wine that's dry but gives the impression of being a bit sweet. Cue a ripe, cherry-flavoured Amarone della Valpolicella.

Sweet chilli/chile
MOSCATO D'ASTI
Sweetness and chilli/chile heat makes for a very tricky wine match, but Moscato d'Asti usually works well. It's floral, with bags of grapey lusciousness and low alcohol, both of which soften the effect of the heat. Plus, even though it's lightly sweet it's usually very crisp so it will cut through the sauce's sticky texture.

Tartare sauce
SAUVIGNON BLANC
The capers and herbs in this sauce are practically screaming 'Pair me with Sauvignon Blanc!' because of this grape's natural affinity with anything heavy in green herbs and saltiness, but you could try a fizz, too.

Salad cream & Thousand Island dressing
RIESLING & PINOT GRIS
The hint of sweetness in off-dry Riesling or Pinot Gris really counters the acidic tang of these sauces.

Tomato ketchup & tomato relish
NEW WORLD PINOT NOIR
These sweet tomato condiments are best with a New World Pinot Noir that's unoaked, so it's plump, juicy, full of raspberry fruit and not too tannic.

Vegemite & Marmite®
OLDER CHAMPAGNE
Seems like a decadent choice, but it's a really great match. Some people might think the dark colour and rich flavour of these spreads needs a red wine, but it's actually the yeasty flavour that you want to match here, and older Champagnes have a rich, yeasty character, while their bubbles prevent the combination from tasting too heavy.

spice

Matching wine with spice isn't always easy and a lot of the places where spicy dishes originate don't have a history of drinking wine, so the world has less experience of matching wine with spice. So, yes, the world of matching wine with spice can be a tricky one, and that world is still a work in progress. But don't despair; there are plenty of grapes, wines and regions that consistently prove they have a natural affinity with dishes that have a kick of spice in them, whether it's the power of paprika, the tang of teriyaki or the joy of ginger.

Indian

Sparkling wine
The light spritz and freshness of fruit in a sparkling wine can actually work brilliantly with lightly dry-spiced seafood dishes like squid, scallops or fried pakora or samosas. Fizz from cooler climates would probably be the best match, like England, Alsace, Germany and Austria.

Moscato d'Asti
This is low in alcohol, very fruity and has sweetness, too, so would be great with any creamy Indian desserts, such as *gulab jaamun* (fried balls of cow's milk), anything fried, or simple dishes without too many spices.

Dry Riesling or Sauvignon Blanc
Dishes that are packed with herbs that have a range of fillings and flavours generally need something aromatic and versatile, like Riesling and Sauvignon Blanc. This includes dishes like saag paneer, momos (the Indian take on dim sum), tandoori chicken, tarka dal and curries with a very rich, creamy sauce.

Off-dry Riesling or off-dry Pinot Gris
This works well with a number of Indian dishes, creamy sauces with fish or white meat, chicken korma and coconut-based curries. Coconut likes an aromatic wine, but can also taste a little bit sweet, which is why you'd go for an off-dry wine rather than one that's fully dry.

Semillon
The subtle apple flavours of young and tangy Australian Semillon make it a great wine for rice dishes that are packed with tons of flavour, spices, nuts, fruit and herbs, like biriyani or kedgeree.

Sherry
Sherry has proven to me on many occasions that it can pair exquisitely with Indian food. I'm talking about dry versions of amontillado, palo cortado and oloroso, especially with rich lentil or tandoori dishes made with red meat or white meats that have been chargrilled.

Dry rosé
A brilliant all-rounder, dry rosé has the best of both worlds, being fresh and crisp with perky acidity. Sometimes it can be quite herbaceous in flavour, which is good for picking up on spice in turmeric-heavy dishes, tomato-based sauce dishes and tarka dal.

Côtes du Rhône or Beaujolais
If it has to be red, these are two pretty good options because they're both fruity and low in tannin, good for tandoori dishes with red meat and all sorts of curries. Very tannic wines won't work with spicy food.

Chinese

Sparkling wine

Super-versatile with food and great for cutting through anything fried, fizz is a great way to start a Chinese meal, whether you're having dim sum or spring rolls. Try the especially crisp ones from England or Austria; and in France, try a Crémant d'Alsace or a Crémant de Loire.

Gewürztraminer

Off-dry Gewürztraminer does a great double-whammy job with Szechuan cuisine – the region that makes the hottest Chinese food. The slight sweetness and intense floral aroma work together to soften the heat and heighten the flavour of strong chilli/chile or ginger-flavoured dishes in Szechuan or Cantonese food.

Riesling

Riesling is especially good with Cantonese food. And here, in the south of China, Cantonese sauces are more subtle than food from the rest of the country, and a wider range of meat and fish is used, too. A Spätlese or an Auslese Riesling from Austria or Germany is a brilliant match with, say, sweet-and-sour pork or chicken, because the sweetness of the wine diminishes the impact of the salt in the dish, and the salt in the dish makes the wine taste less sweet. Plus the fruit in the dish has a juicy wine to stand up to it. Dry Riesling like a German Kabinett or one from South Australia, is also great at the start of the meal, with dim sum or steamed fish and shellfish.

Pinot Noir & Merlot

Tannin is the enemy of spicy food, so avoid it if you can. Instead, you want lots of juicy fruit, which you can get with either of these grapes, although the New World might be a better option because it scores higher on the 'plump and juicy' scale. These red wines are great with dishes from the west of China, where richer meats like duck and beef are more common. Pinot Noir is especially delicious with Peking duck, for example. These also work with dishes like Cantonese beef with tomatoes, as well as a soy-based meat dish. Then there's black bean sauce, and coatings like those you find on sticky Chinese ribs, both of which would need a plump but not overpowering glass of red.

Japanese

Champagne

I've specified Champagne here rather than any other sparkling wine because the intricacy of flavour and complexity found in Champagne are a very good match with the umami and spice in Japanese food. A fresh and young Blanc de Blancs is great with things like shoyu ramen, which has the freshness of spring onions/scallions, bamboo shoots and beansprouts. Plus, it works with tempura. Aged Champagnes seem to make a scandalously (expensively!) good match with sushi and sashimi that's been doused in soy sauce.

Mineral dry whites

The fresh, salty flavour of the sea in these wines is fantastic with an array of Japanese food, especially when there's seaweed. The best salt-friendly wines are Sauvignon Blanc, Friulano, Muscadet and fino or manzanilla Sherry.

Riesling & Gewürztraminer

Riesling is a delicious match with teriyaki sauce on fish and white meat, and it's great with the ginger and garlic, too. Although, any dish with ginger loves the rose petal and ginger-flavoured Gewürz.

Beaujolais

A versatile red with many Japanese dishes, thanks to its upfront, red-berry flavours. This is especially useful with soy sauce, which isn't the easiest of flavours, with its salty, dense taste.

New Zealand Pinot Noir

You really want cherry and raspberry fruit to sing out with Japanese food, so a New Zealand Pinot Noir, that isn't too heavy on tannin, is a fantastic choice with beef teriyaki and yakitori. It is also the winning choice with Japan's killer seven-spice shichimi, which is often sprinkled on top of noodle dishes.

Thai

Riesling

Riesling gets the all-round gold medal with Thai food. A fruity, zesty Riesling, with all its lemon and lime flavours, works a treat with the ingredients in Thai salads like shallots, mint, coriander/cilantro, lemongrass, lime juice, and peanuts. A richer Riesling would have the mettle to stand up to Thai stir-fried vegetables. It's probably the best match with Thai curries, of the green and red variety, too.

Grüner Veltliner

Austria's darling grape is the perfect match for the fresh and vibrant flavours in a Thai salad. The GVs we're now seeing from New Zealand are especially worth trying because of their extra hint of tropicality.

Sparkling wine

For anything fried, bring in a sparkling wine. My favourite option with Thai food, Moscato d'Asti, is hard to beat. This super-fruity, low alcohol, slightly fizzy, slightly sweet wine picks up on the zesty flavours in the food, cuts through fried food like crab cakes, lifts the fruity flavour in the meat of pink shellfish like crab and prawns/shrimps, and can even cut through the richness and depth of flavour in Pad Thai.

Barbera

If you really, really, *really* have to go for a red wine because you want it with red meat, then this low-tannin, high in natural acid red grape from Italy is the answer.

Caribbean

Sparkling wine
Fresh and zippy acidity is the hallmark of sparkling wines, which are not only versatile wines for all dishes, but also with freshly fried fish and snacks, like accra.

Rosé
Jerk seasoning is the ultimate wine challenge, because it has a powerful combination of garlic, hot chilli/chile pepper, allspice, nutmeg and cinnamon, and probably lots of other ingredients, too. A punchy rosé from Navarra is fantastic because it's usually made with Garnacha, which is a low-tannin red grape.

Mexican

Cabernet Franc, French Syrah, Sangiovese or herbal whites
Chimichurri – made with dry spices, fresh herbs and garlic – with steak is a winner with wines that can show herbal flavours: Cabernet Franc or a Syrah blend from the south of France. If the herbal-heavy chimichurri is paired with fish or chicken, herbal white wines – like a Sauvignon Blanc from Sancerre, a Loureiro from Portugal, a Vermentino from Italy or an Albariño from Spain – are great.

Malbec or Carmenère
For pure, unadulterated wine pleasure with Mexican red meat, either of South America's signature red grapes are excellent.

Italian reds
Wraps like fajitas and burritos are packed with flavour and attitude, so with these I like a softer, juicier red wine and that usually takes me to Italy, with those cherry-filled wines like Sangiovese or Montepulciano.

Zinfandel
Being both fruity and earthy, Zinfandel makes a great match with mole sauce, as well as anything with a significant amount of chipotle in the recipe. It's also great with chili con carne and milder Tex-Mex dishes.

Dry rosé
As long as the rosé is fresh and not too wimpy in flavour, it can work with fish tacos, ceviche, and spicy shellfish, chorizo and chicken.

Crisp & fruity whites
There are so many versions of this style, they go with anything from Mexican rice with chicken, ceviche, chicken empanadas, tomato salsa and even guacamole. Top of my shopping list is Sauvignon Blanc, Albariño, Vinho Verde, white Douro wines and Grüner Veltliner.

North African & Eastern Mediterranean

Dry rosé
Of all the spicy dishes a dry rosé can match, it comes into its own with this style of cooking. Everything bar red meat dishes work. Rosés from Bandol, Tavel or Provence are happy with strong spices like *ras el hanout*, sumac and harissa, and go with lighter chicken tagines.

Lebanese or Moroccan red
With red-meat dishes, lamb especially, with its spice, nuts and dried fruit, the local reds with earthy spiciness match well. These styles are also great with aubergine/eggplant in dishes like baba ganoush. The softness of Lebanese Merlot is preferable here. Morocco, meanwhile, is doing an increasingly good job with the lovely fragrant red grape Carignan. If you struggle to find either of those, Sicilian Nero d'Avola is a tasty alternative.

Time for takeout

Even if we've taken the easy option for a meal and got someone else to make it for us, we still want a decent wine to match, so here are a few of my top takeout food wines in no particular order.

What should I drink with pizza?
ROSSO DI MONTEPULCIANO
These wines are Tuscan classics, fragrant but score highly on the juicy scale. I like their mellow character with rich pizzas.

CHIANTI
A name we're all familiar with, this is easy to find. Full of cherry fruit flavours and good for pizza of all kinds, whether vegetarian or meat.

RED LAMBRUSCO
This is what some of the coolest pizza restaurants serve as their go-to pizza-matching wine. It's slightly fizzy, which gives the ripe fruit extra freshness to cut through the fat of the cheese or a meat topping.

BEAUJOLAIS
If you're going non-Italian, a ripe and fruity Beaujolais is always a good choice, because it's fresh enough to cut through the richness of the pizza toppings.

What should I drink with fish & chips?
ENGLISH SPARKLING WINE
Fizz and fried food is a great pairing but it feels pleasingly extravagant. English sparkling wine has an extra edge of freshness to its appley flavour that cuts straight through the oil of the food.

CHAMPAGNE
The best style is usually a Blanc de Blancs, exclusively made from Chardonnay. These are typically more floral and lighter on their feet than other Champagne styles, which again, cut through the grease.

SAUVIGNON BLANC
There are three reasons why a zingy Sauvignon Blanc works: the acidity is good for the batter, the grass and herbaceous characters are made for mouth- puckering tartare sauce, and the green flavours win with mushy peas.

FINO OR MANZANILLA SHERRY
Another wine made by the sea. Salty, and completely dry, these fresh and crisp wines work with the fish especially well and are fantastic with batter.

What should I drink with fried chicken?
CHAMPAGNE OR PROSECCO
You can go one of two ways with fizz for fried chicken. You can go light with pear-flavoured Prosecco, which lifts the grease of the chicken, or you can go richer with a toasty Champagne, which is at one with the batter.

RIESLING
Ever the versatile food grape, Riesling also cuts a mean streak of freshness through the richness of fried chicken. A slightly off-dry wine offers sweetness to pair with the sweet and salty flavour of the chicken.

CHARDONNAY
The melon flavour of unoaked Chardonnay goes with the meat, whereas oaked Chardonnay has the mellow, buttery richness to match the batter.

cheese

The intoxicating aroma of cheese is like a homing beacon for we wine drinkers. Not just because wine and cheese have a natural affinity and enhance each other's flavours, but because they share humble origins and complex flavours. The world of wine-and-cheese matching has changed in recent years. Gone are the days of choosing red by default; instead, it's white wine that's making some of the most sublime and successful cheese matches, and that's all down to acidity.

Want to know more? Well, our perception of acidity in white wines is higher, making it a great partner to the fatty content of cheese. As a general guide, soft cheeses and strong flavours are great with fresh white wines; hard cheese and milder flavours have a better chance of pairing well with rich white wines; and the more pungent the cheese, the sweeter the wine should be. Of course red wines have acidity too, which means we shouldn't rule out red wine completely – I'm just saying that, on the whole, white wine is more versatile, and therefore more likely to match different cheeses better. So, here are a few ideas to get started, while over the next few pages I've included flights of cheeses grouped by country, together with some of their tasty local wine pairings.

Hard cheese
CHEDDAR, COMTÉ, EDAM, FONTINA, GRUYÈRE, MANCHEGO, PARMESAN & RED LEICESTER

The richness of flavour in a mature hard cheese like a Cheddar or Gruyère usually calls for a white wine with guts and depth of flavour. In which case, there a few grape varieties in my mind that have the potential to work well. They're all white grapes that are delicious when they're a bit older: a dry Gewurztraminer, preferably from Alsace; a Viognier; a Chardonnay, such as an aged Premier Cru Chablis or a Californian with light oakiness; a Semillon, like an aged Hunter Semillon; or, if possible, Chenin Blanc.

Alternatively, you could try a *vin jaune*. This is a French wine from the Jura region and has a richness of flavour, texture and a fresh, salty tang to it, great with something like the concentrated, intense Comté, also from Jura. If the hard cheese is mild, like Edam, then pick a younger white or try a different grape. Something like a good Pinot Blanc from Alsace is a great and quite versatile with all kinds of different cheeses. Meanwhile, I've always liked Red Leicester with dry red wine, as long as it's smooth and elegant.

Fortified wines

Some of these are brilliant with the salt, tang and fruitiness of mature hard cheeses. Dry Sherries, such as palo cortado or amontillado, would be superb with cheese, or if you want Madeira, try a little drop of Verdelho Madeira. When it comes to Port, there's nothing better than a slightly chilled Tawny Port. For more information on fortified wines see pages 116–121.

Soft cheese
BRIE, CAMEMBERT & TALEGGIO

With cheeses that stick to your mouth, like Camembert and Brie, I prefer white wines that cut through the stickiness. The cheese-versatile Pinot Blanc is a winner, or you could pick a fresh Chardonnay style that's rounded without being too oaky or heavy, like Chablis (but not the Premier Cru and Grand Cru styles). Some friends swear by red wines with these sorts of cheeses, so if that's your preference, I'd keep it light with a grape like Pinot Noir, Cabernet Franc, maybe even Barbera, or, perhaps the best option, Gamay, because the fruit is refreshing and the level of tannin is low.

Goat's cheese

Step forward Sauvignon Blanc. It's a universal fact that goat's cheese and Sauvignon Blanc are a match made in heaven. My 'wow' moment with this pairing actually happened in Durbanville, South Africa, when a group of producers pulled together a lunch tasting menu of goat's cheese with a range of Sauvignon Blancs from local producers – it blew me away.

Any unoaked Sauvignon Blanc will work well with goat's cheese, but I find there's something about high-quality, freshly-mown-grass-smelling South African
and Chilean Sauvignon Blancs that have a special synergy with goat's cheese. If you like New Zealand Sauv Blancs, don't go for the very tropical, passion fruit-flavoured ones as this might overwhelm goat's cheese – try something a little mellower.

Dry Riesling is also widely touted as a good match for goat's cheese, and it genuinely is. But, for me, it's never quite achieved the same dizzy heights with goat's cheese as Sauvignon Blanc.

Blue cheese
DANISH BLUE, DOLCELATTE, GORGONZOLA, ROQUEFORT & STILTON
Sweet wines

Many people follow the school of thought that a very pungent blue cheese needs a massive red table wine to stand up to it, when in actual fact a pungent blue cheese would stop even the biggest of dry reds dead in its tracks. From Roquefort to Gorgonzola to Stilton, the no-brainer match for salty pungent blue cheese is actually a sweet wine. France, of course, has these in spades. Sauternes from Bordeaux is a good option, but might be out of some people's price bracket. Usually a blend of Sauvignon Blanc, Semillon and/or Muscadelle, its mesmerizing honeyed sweetness cuts through (and

enhances) the pungency of blue cheeses perfectly. A delicious and underrated French option is Pacherenc du Vic-Bilh (shorten it to 'Pacherenc' to keep things simple). This is made in Madiran in south-west France from local grapes Gros Manseng and Petit Manseng. With an especially rich cheese you could treat yourself to a heavenly Tokaji from Hungary, and then there's Port, too! I know it's red but I wouldn't want to totally rule out Port, because the wine's sweetness will carry through the cheese's pungency. That said, luscious sticky whites are a more natural bedfellow with full-on cheese, but they don't just have to come from Europe. From the southern hemisphere, late- harvest and botrytis wines made with Sauvignon Blanc or Semillon (or both together) would also be great.

cheese & pasta

Another way cheese stakes its claim on our palate is in cheesy pasta sauces. The sauce of a dish may be the dominant flavour, so take care when pairing wine with dishes where cheese wins out. Here are a few tips to get started.

Wine style	Grape
Italian white	Ribolla Gialla, Curtefranca, white Franciacorta
Non-Italian white	Chardonnay
Red	Merlot

A taste of France

When it comes to both cheese and wine, France basks in the glory of being most people's spiritual home, even though it has way more competition for world-class wine these days than it does for world-class cheese. Given that cheese and wine production are so prolific, and the results are often of such high quality, a simple – but usually effective – guide is to keep things local. That's to say, drink a local French wine with a cheese from the same region and the outcome is likely to be a melt-in-the-mouth experience.

BRIE & LOIRE ROSÉ (OPPOSITE, LEFT)

Brie is a sticky cow's milk cheese that's hugely popular, although it isn't always the easiest cheese to pair with wine because it can range from being mild and chalky when young to being rich and gooey when mature. A fruity wine with crisp acidity is the way to go, so if you can get over the snobbery aspect that surrounds pink wines with cheese, a dry rosé is a great choice here. It's versatile enough to go with either style of cheese and the ultimate pairing would be a dry Cabernet Franc rosé from the Loire Valley, which is zingy and fruity, and has enough bite to cut straight through sticky Brie.

★ COMTÉ & ALSACE PINOT GRIS (OPPOSITE, CENTRE)

Borough Market in London is to thank for many Londoners' (like me) love affair with Comté because there's a stall there dedicated to nothing but this ripe and firm, hard cheese from the Jura region of France. Although the rind is very hard, the texture inside is smooth, and the beauty of Comté is its range of deep flavours, which can be anything from nutty and creamy to fruity, peppery and toasty. This, therefore, calls for a rich white, and yet not one that's too overpowering in flavour. That leads me straight to a dry Pinot Gris from Alsace, which can be rich in weight but pretty in flavour. It's very smooth, so it glides along the smooth cheese in you mouth – it's gorgeously moreish!

Pinot Gris has been made internationally famous by its Italian sibling, Pinot Grigio. But when it's Pinot Gris, as it is in Alsace, France (and other parts of the World), the overall effect is usually a textured wine usually with a ripe, honeyed, pear flavour.

Of course, coming from Jura, Comté also pairs incredibly well with a *vin jaune* from the same region.

ROQUEFORT & SAUTERNES (OPPOSITE, RIGHT)

Roquefort is a blue cheese made from sheep's milk in the south of France. Nicknamed the 'cheese of kings and popes', it's one of the products alongside red wine that's thought to contribute to that French Paradox theory: that the French live longer despite the rich food in their diet. Flavour-wise, Roquefort can be both creamy and sharp, tangy and salty, and of course, it's rich in flavour. Nothing highlights all of this better than an elegant sticky, sweet wine like Sauternes, which is my ultimate match. The days of pairing Roquefort with red wine are long gone.

While I say Sauternes, if I went really specific, I'd say Barsac, which is a wine appellation that actually lies within the appellation of Sauternes. There is very little to tell them apart, other than to say, very generally, that Sauternes is richer than Barsac, which is seen as more elegant. They'd be equally delicious with Roquefort, though, so I'd give them both a go!

A taste of England

On a daily basis the French and Italians eat about twice as much cheese as the English do, but even so, the artisan cheese industry is thriving in England, and has been since the early 1990s. Oh, and haven't you heard about its wine industry? That's now thriving, too, and not just the sparkling wine but still table wines are improving all the time as well. Yes, England may be the new-ish kid on the block for quality wine and quality cheese, but it's definitely one worth checking out.

GOAT'S CHEESE & ENGLISH BACCHUS (OPPOSITE, LEFT)

Okay, okay, I know I've waxed lyrical about the wonders of goat's cheese with Sauvignon Blanc earlier in this section, but my excuse is that Bacchus is England's answer to Sauvignon Blanc! A successful wine match with goat's cheese is really down to the characteristics of the grape, which needs to make a wine that's light on its feet as well as fruity and often grassy in flavour. And this is right up Bacchus' street, because as far as cheese goes, goat's cheese shares all of these flavours: it's grassy, clean and has a tangy bite to it.

England is one of the best countries for Bacchus, partly because it has a cool climate and this is a low-acidity grape, so the English versions don't taste too tart. It's very fruity, and when you serve it alongside a fresh green salad with goat's cheese and that other very English ingredient, asparagus, it's a wine and food match that's hard to beat.

WENSLEYDALE & ENGLISH PINOT NOIR (OPPOSITE, CENTRE)

A crumbly cow's milk cheese made in the north of England, Wensleydale is known for its milky freshness and chalky texture. It can come plain or blended with other ingredients, and in either case it's a winner with English Pinot Noir, because even though this is a red wine, it's a super-fresh red with bright raspberry and beetroot/beet flavours. It's also low in tannin, which all combines brilliantly to cut through the creamy flavour and chalky texture of Wensleydale. This is never more true than when the cheese is dotted with cranberries, as it often is.

English Pinot Noir is growing in popularity and quality and it's increasingly being found in England, although this is because it's now such a key ingredient in the English sparkling wine scene.

CHEDDAR & ENGLISH SPARKLING WINE (OPPOSITE, RIGHT)

I could hardly not talk about English fizz now, could I? It's becoming an iconic, world-renowned sparkling wine in its own right, and luckily for cheese-lovers, the high-quality English sparkling wines have enough flavour and personality to work brilliantly with Cheddar. Historically, Cheddar has been paired with Chardonnay, especially those from Chablis, so it only makes sense that sparkling wine from England, also made from Chardonnay, should work. It has an extra-toasty flavour to it, thanks to the enriching process of sparkling winemaking.

The absolute perfect marriage would be a Chardonnay-only (sometimes called Blanc de Blancs) English sparkling wine that's a slightly older vintage. I appreciate this may be harder to track down because the industry is still relatively young, but if you can get it, do. If you can't, don't worry, the inherently English apple flavour that comes with top-notch English sparkling wine is always going to be a winner with Cheddar anyway.

A taste of Italy

Italy is a melting pot of identities and cultures, and its historic fragmentation is reflected in its cheeses, which are hugely varied in style and flavour. This fragmentation of course is also obvious when you look at Italy's fruit salad of grapes and wine styles, even if certain grapes are now shared between regions. As with France, a basic but useful Italian cheese-and-wine matching guide is to look at products that come from the same region.

GRANA PADANO & FRANCIACORTA (OPPOSITE, LEFT)

Grana Padano was exclusively used as a garnish for my pasta before I visited the region of Franciacorta. When there, one of the local winemakers welcomed me with an aperitif of Franciacorta served alongside some knobbly lumps of 24-month aged Grana Padano. What a revelation! It wasn't just the flavour combination that was immense, but it reminded me that good Grana Padano should see the light of day in its own right as a cheese, and should more often be served with nibbles – in the same way Manchego is served as a tapas dish.

The success of this pairing is firstly about texture. Although the cheese is crumbly when you cut it, it's pretty waxy in the mouth, and this matches perfectly with the bubbles in Franciacorta. Especially so with the style Satèn, which has lower pressure and therefore softer bubbles, made even more mellow with the texture of the cheese. There's also a synergy with flavour between these. Both the wine and cheese here are slightly nutty and fruity, although as with most wine and cheese matches, the older the cheese, the better an older Franciacorta would work. If you don't want sparkling wine, try the still Chardonnay made in Franciacorta called Curtefranca. If you can't get hold of Grana Padano, then it would also work brilliantly with Parmigiano-Reggiano.

TALEGGIO & BARBERA (OPPOSITE, CENTRE)

Taleggio is a squidgy washed-rind cheese made from the curds of cow's milk across northern Italy. Usually on a cheese counter at your local supermarket or deli, you can also find it cut into squares. This cheese has a mild flavour and fruitiness, but its trademark character is a nutty, earthy aroma, a bit similar to how soil smells after it's been raining. Despite how that sounds, it's actually a divine cheese and one of my all-time favourites. A classic and unbeatable match here is the red Piedmontese grape, Barbera, which is high in acid and low in tannin: fresh enough to cut through the squidgy texture of the cheese. When it comes to flavour, Barbera often has that truffley, earthy smell that works perfectly, too. But if you don't drink red wine, try a northern Italian Pinot Bianco instead.

MOZZARELLA & ROSATO (OPPOSITE, RIGHT)

This is a perfect example of matching the old with the new. Mozzarella di Bufala is a fresh, unripened cheese that's a stretched, or pulled, curd cheese. It dates back to the 12th century and tastes full of milky goodness. Meanwhile, although the world can't get enough of rosé wine, it's still not given nearly enough credit as a versatile food wine. When it's dry, it's delicious with this cheese, and especially good when it comes from the south of Italy (which is also the home to Mozzarella di Bufala) in Puglia, using the local grape Negroamaro. The creamy texture of the cheese is delicious with the freshness of the wine, while strawberry and cream flavours in the rosé pick up the creamy flavour of the mozzarella. And as if this weren't an enticing enough match, mozzarella is sometimes at its best when served with tomatoes, which also work brilliantly with rosé. But if rosé really is a no-no, then try a nutty-flavoured Italian white grape variety like Falanghina.

A taste of Spain

Manchego is synonymous with Spanish cheese for many people, and as delicious as it is, Spain's cheese scene is just as diverse as that of its wine. Spanish cheese is generally classified as light, medium or strong in flavour, and when it comes to origin, you can also see a broad pattern emerge: cow's milk cheeses are more common in the north of the country, sheep's milk cheeses come from more inland quarters, while goat's milk cheeses are found along the Mediterranean coastline. And thankfully, Spain isn't short on the number of wines to work with these cheesy delights. Olé!

MANCHEGO & FINO SHERRY (OPPOSITE, LEFT)

Spain's most famous cheese is semi-hard and made with thick Manchego sheep milk in La Mancha, the hot, landlocked interior of Spain. The richness of the milk gives Manchego its delectable nutty flavour, and although the age of it (and therefore depth of flavour) can vary, it's a no-brainer match with tapas at the start of a meal. And that only calls for one kind of wine: Sherry.

Sherry is Manchego's soulmate, particularly fino, the lightest style of Sherry you can find, and one that's always bone-dry. Just as dry (if not more) than your average white wine, in fact, and it even looks like a bright white wine in the glass. Fino has a pretty, floral aromatic delicacy, while it's zesty, salty and very refreshing in the mouth. Its almond flavour is also a great counterpart to the nuttiness of Manchego.

PICOS BLUE & SWEET MOSCATEL (OPPOSITE, CENTRE)

A smooth and creamy blue cheese, Picos Blue comes from the mountainous area in northern Spain known as Picos Europa or Valdéon, which is also the name of the town it comes from. It's a cow's milk cheese that is wrapped in vine or maple leaves. It sometimes has goat's milk added to it, but this is only done at certain times of the year, when goat's milk is available. It's a tangy and sometimes spicy blue cheese that's milder and more crumbly when it's younger. Because the flavour is rich and intense, a Spanish dessert wine made from Moscatel (known as 'Muscat' elsewhere in the world) is the way to go.

Moscatel is a very classic grape used in the production of Spanish sweet wines. They are luscious wines with flavours of oranges and toasted nuts, put together with a streak of rich honey that is just perfect to glide over the tang and spice of this Spanish blue cheese. Historically you'll also see this cheese recommended with red wine, but sweet wine is the best match in my book.

TETILLA & GODELLO (OPPOSITE, RIGHT)

Tetilla means 'small breast' in Spanish, and the cheese is given this name because of its very, er, identifiable dome shape. This is a cow's milk creamy cheese that hails from Galicia in north-west Spain and it has a number of names, often with the word *teta* included. The creamy texture is its hallmark, making it quite a popular stuffing cheese, especially because it melts easily. When the flavours are kept simple, it's a genius match with a local Galician white, Godello.

Just as Tetilla is soft and gentle, so, too, is Godello, which is really supple on the palate. This grape is quickly moving up the ranks in reputation in the wine world, and makes a juicy, slightly peachy-flavoured wine, especially in the Galician region of Valdeorras.

resources

BOOKS

Niki Segnit
The Flavour Thesaurus
(Bloomsbury, 2010)

Jancis Robinson, Julia Harding and
José Vouillamoz
Wine Grapes
(Allen Lane, 2012)

Hugh Johnson and Jancis Robinson
The World Atlas of Wine
(Mitchell Beazley, 2013)

Tom Stevenson and Essi Avellan
*World Encyclopedia of Champagne &
Sparkling Wine*
(Absolute Press, 2013)

Jancis Robinson
The Oxford Companion to Wine
(Oxford University Press, 2006)

ONLINE
Liv–ex
www.liv-ex.com
An invaluable source of information if
you're interested in wine investment.

Vinography
www.vinography.com
A useful and informative North
American-based blog.

The Wine Gang
www.thewinegang.com (but, of course!)
To find out which wines to buy in the
UK.

Wine–Searcher and The
Wine Web
www.wine-searcher.com
www.wineweb.com
To track down where a wine is sold.

MAGAZINES
Decanter
www.decanter.com
A UK-based consumer wine magazine's
site with tips, news and regional
reports.

World of Fine Wine
www.worldoffinewine.com
A UK-based wine magazine's site with
in-depth and cerebral wine articles.

Wine Enthusiast
www.winemag.com
A USA-based wine magazine with
reviews, news and recipes too.

RETAILERS
Berry Bros. & Rudd
www.bbr.com
A great wine merchant in the UK with a
website packed with information.

EuroCave
www.eurocave.co.uk
A UK-based one-stop shop for glasses,
decanters, wine chillers and all kinds of
wine paraphernalia.

The Wine Society
www.thewinesociety.com
A great wine merchant in the UK with a
website packed with information.

index

Abadía Retuerta 53
ageing 14, 41, 74, 85, 92, 100, 119, 120
Agiorgitiko 65, 134
Aglianico 9
Airén 112
Albariño 70, 110, 142
alcohol levels 31, 46, 49, 56, 57, 65, 99, 116, 121, 125
Alheit, Chris 91
Alvarinho 10, 154
Anjou 91
Aragonez 52
Argentina 60

Arneis 9, 108
aromatics 82, 104, 107
Assyrtiko 145
Ata Rangi 29
Ausbruch 125
Auslese 11, 115, 125
Australia
  Adelaide Hills 86
  Barossa Valley 34, 49
  Clare Valley 94, 102
  Coonawarra 38
  Eden Valley 75, 102
  Hunter Valley 94
  Langhorne Creek 49, 60

Margaret River 34, 38, 60, 94
McLaren Vale 10, 34, 49
Mornington Peninsula 80
Rutherglen 94, 99, 115, 120
Tasmania 80, 129
Austria
  Burgenland 125
  Wachau 102
Auxerrois 58

Bacchus 146, 166
Badenhorst, Adi 91
Banyuls 120, 149

barbecues 69, 132
Barbera 24, 54, 57, 169
Barsac 84, 92, 94, 122, 164
Beaujolais 87, 156, 160, 161
Beaujolais Nouveau 31, 64
Beck, Graham 129
Beerenauslese 11, 115, 125
Bellavista 78, 129
Bellingham 62
Bergstrom 29
Berlucchi, Fratelli 78, 129
biodynamic wine 81, 91
Blanc de Blancs 78, 128, 142
Blanc de Noirs 26, 128

Blaufränkisch 24, 65
blends 10, 34, 36, 38, 42, 44, 46, 50, 66, 91, 92, 112
Bobal 31, 53
Bollinger 69
Bonarda 134
Bordeaux classifications 11
botrytis 86, 94, 122, 125
Bott-Geyl 102
Bourboulenc 48
Brachetto 115
Brazil 129
Brunello 56
Brut 21, 128
Bulgaria 30
Burn Cottage 30
bush vine 46

Cabernet Franc 24, 25, 31, 36, 44, 66, 159
Cabernet Sauvignon 24, 25, 32, 36–40, 44, 53, 57, 68, 82
cakes, vegetable 149
Campbells 94
Cannonau 46, 49
Carbernet Franc 36
Carignan 9, 46, 48, 49, 66
Carignano 49
Cariñena 49
Carmenère 24, 44, 62, 68, 159
Carricante 108
Casa Lapostolle 40
Casa Real 29
Casa Silver 86
Castello del Terricio 40
Cava 78, 112, 113, 115, 126
cellar cold 31
Cencibel 52
Chablis 78, 139, 140
Chacolí/Txacoli 112
Champagne 21, 87, 126
   food with 115, 142, 155, 160, 161
   rosé 69, 139
   vintage 128, 139
Chardonnay 21, 71, 76–80, 113, 124, 126, 128, 129, 144, 161
Chateau Ste Michelle 102
cheese 162–170
Chenin Blanc 71, 88–91, 124,

129, 144
Chianti 161
Chile 29, 31, 34, 60, 86
chilling red wine 29, 31
China 10, 38, 40
choosing wine 24-5, 70-1, 114-5
Churton 75
Cinsaut 32, 46, 48, 62, 66
Clairette 48
Clairette de Die 99
Clonakilla 34
Clos Clare 102
Cloudy Bay 84
Coates & Seely 69, 78, 129
Códax, Martín 110
Codega 118
Colheita 118
Colombard 91
Cono Sur 29
cork removal 16
Corvina 57, 127
Cot/Côt 58
Coteaux du Layon 124
Coterno 54
Côtes du Rhone 156
Courbu Blanc *see* Hondarrabi Zuri
Craggy Range 29, 84
Crémant 87, 115, 126, 129
Cristom 29
Croatia 62, 65, 145
Crus *see* quality hierarchies
Cullen Wines 34
Curtefranca 78, 163, 169

Dampt, Vincent 78
De Lucca 65
De Martino 40, 64
decanting 16–17, 118
Delamotte 78
Delaporte, Vincent 30
dessert wine *see* sweet wine
Deutz 78
Digby Fine English 69
Doctors Flat 30
Dog Point 30, 84
Dolcetto 24
Domaine Drouhin 29
Dosnon & Lepage 69
Dry Creek Vineyard 91

È Solo 107
Efest 102
eggs 150–1
Einaudi, Poderi 99
Eiswein 11, 125
England 69, 78, 115, 126, 129, 161, 166
Eradus 107
Errázuriz 40
Etna Rosso 56, 57, 135

Fairtrade® wines 81
Falanghina 108, 154, 169
Fantino 54
Felton Road 30
Ferrari-Carano 84
Fessy, Henry 64
Fiano 108
fish 139–145, 161
fizz *see* sparkling wine
foil cutting 16
Forrester, Ken 91
fortified wine 116–21
   Australian 99, 115, 120
   food with 115, 119–20, 170
   Portuguese 115, 116, 118, 149
   Spanish 115, 119–20, 121, 156, 161, 170
The Foundry 75
France
   Alsace 11, 30, 99, 102, 104, 107, 122, 164
   Beaujolais 64
   Bergerac 36, 94
   Bonnezeaux 124
   Bordeaux 11, 38, 42, 84, 92, 122
   Burgundy 11, 26, 76
   Cahors 58
   Chablis 78
   Champagne 11, 66, 78, 128
   Châteauneuf-du-Pape 32, 48
   Condrieu 72
   Corbiéres 48
   Côte de Beaune 26, 76
   Côte de Nuits 26
   Coteaux du Layon 124
   Côtes Catalanes 48
   Côtes du Rhône 48
   Faugères 48
   Fitou 48

Gigondas 32, 48
   Jura 124, 162
   Languedoc-Roussillon 9, 48, 75
   Loire Valley 30, 66, 82, 84, 88, 124, 164
   Marcillac 31
   Minervois 48
   Provence 66
   Quarts-de-Chaume 124
   Rhône Valley 32, 48, 72, 75, 99
   Roussillon 99
   Saint Chinian 48
   Savennières 88
   South-west France 31, 36, 124
   Tavel 48
   Vacqueyras 48
Franciacorta 78, 115, 126, 129, 163, 169
Frappato 31
Friulano 9, 108
Fumé Blanc 84
Furmint 124

Gaia 65
Gamay 24, 64
game 137–8
Garganega 143, 154
Garnacha 46, 49, 68
Garnacha Blanca 112
Garnaxta 46
Germany
   Baden 29, 30
   Mosel 100
   Pfalz 29
Gewürztraminer 71, 96, 104, 122, 158, 160
Giera 126, 129
Giesen 80
glassware 18–21
Godello 9, 53, 71, 110, 142, 170
Graciano 53
Gramona 113
Gran Reserva 11
Grange Cochard, Ch. 64
Greece 65, 96, 99
Grenache 9, 24, 25, 31, 32, 46–9, 66
Grenache Blanc 48
Grenache Noir 120

Groot Constantia 62
Gros Manseng 124, 163
Grosset 102
Grüner Veltliner 71, 102, 140
GSM 46, 49
Gusbourne 69, 129

The Hay Paddock 34
Hedge's 38
Heinrich, Gernot & Heike 65
Hermitage see Cinsaut
Hiedsieck, Charles 69, 78
Hondarrabi Zuri 112
Huet, Dom. 88
Hugel 99, 102, 107
Hungary 30, 124

icewine 115, 122, 125
Iona 86
Isabel Estate 84, 107
Israel 46, 49
Italy
    Abruzzo 56
    Amarone 57
    Barbaresco 54, 57
    Barolo 54, 57
    Campania 9
    Central 108
    Chianti 54, 57
    Franciacorta 78, 126, 129
    Friuli 69, 84, 106, 107, 108
    Marche 108
    Montalcino 56
    Piedmont 9, 54, 99, 108,
        124
    Prosecco 115, 129
    Puglia 9, 56, 62, 68
    Salice Salentini 68
    Sardinia 46, 108
    Sicily 56, 108, 125
    Tuscany 40, 54, 56, 108,
        124
    Valpolicella 57
    Veneto 57, 107, 125

Jackson Estate 84
Jacob's Creek 129
Jansz 80, 129
Januik 80
Jasper Hill 34
Jenkyn Place 69, 129
Jermann 107

Joly, Nicolas 88
Josmeyer 107
Juanicó 65
Jurançon 124

K Vintners 34
Kabinett 11
Katnook 34
Knoll, Weingut 102
Kumeu River 80

labelling wine 9, 11, 26, 46, 76
Lambrusco 31, 161
Langhe Nebbiolo 54
Lanzarote 113
Larmandier-Bernier 78
Late Bottled Vintage 118
late harvest 99, 102, 115, 122,
    125
Lebanon 160
lees 76, 88, 126
Leeuwin Estate 80
Lehman, Peter 129
Leonetti Cellars 34
Léoube, Ch. 66
light wines 24, 25
liqueur de tirage 128
Liqueur Muscat 99
Loosen, Ernie 102
Loureiro 10
Lupicaia 40

Macabeo see Viura
Madeira 115, 120, 149
Madiran 36, 64, 65, 124, 163
making wine 64, 66, 76, 86,
    126
Malbec 24, 25, 44, 58-61, 68,
    159
Malmsey 120
Malvasia 112, 113, 120
Malvasia Bianca 124
Mann, Albert 102
Mansois 31
Marimar Estate 80
Marques de Casa Concha 64
Marsala 115
Marsanne 135, 150
Masi 107
Mataro 49
Maury 120
Mazuelo see Carignan

meat 132-9
Mediterranean food 159-60
Mencía 9, 31, 53
Meritage blend 44
Merlot 24, 25, 36, 38, 40,
    42-5, 57, 58, 62, 68, 158
Mi Sueno 80
Millton Vineyard 91
Miroglio, Edoardo 30
Molinara 57, 125
Monastrell see Mourvèdre
Monbazillac 94, 115, 124
Mondavi, Robert 84
Monte Rossa 78
Montepulciano 24, 56
Moreau-Naudet 78
Morin, Gérard et Pierre 30
Morocco 46, 160
Moscatel 96, 119, 170
Moscato 96
Moscato d'Asti 99, 115, 124-5,
    155, 156
Moschato 96
Mount Edward 30
Mourvèdre 32, 46, 48, 49
Mullineux 91
Muscadelle 84, 94, 122, 124
Muscat 70, 96-9, 115, 120, 122
Muscat Blanc à Petit Grains
    96, 99

natural wine 81
Nebbiolo 24, 41, 54, 57
Negroamaro 9, 25
Nerello Cappuccio 56, 57
Nerello Mascalese 56, 57
Nero d'Avola 10, 56
Nero di Troia 9
Neudorf 84
New Zealand
    Central Otago 29, 102
    Hawke's Bay 10, 34, 75
    Marlborough 30, 84, 102
    Martinborough 29, 75
    Waiheke Island 10, 34
    Waipara Valley 102
Ngatarawa 80
noble rot see botrytis
Noval, Quinta do 65
Nyetimber 78, 129

oak 38, 41, 71, 76, 84, 85

old vines 94, 120
opening wine 16
organic wine 66, 81
Ornellaia 57
Ott, Dom. 66

Palacios, Rafael 110
Palladius 91
Parellada 113
party wines 87
Pasqua 107
Passito de Pantelleria 125
Paumanok Vineyards 91
Pazo de Señorans 110
Pecorino 108
Pegasus Bay 102
Peregrine 102
Perrone, Elio 99
Pesquera 53
Petit Courbu 124
Petit Manseng 124, 163
Petit Verdot 44
Pewsey Vale 102
Picardan 48
picnic wines 69
pink wine 26, 58, 62, 66, 68,
    69, 87, 118, 128
    see also rosé
Pinot Beurot 104
Pinot Bianco 129
Pinot Blanc 26
Pinot Grigio 70, 104-7, 155
Pinot Grigio Ramato 69
Pinot Gris 26, 71, 107, 156,
    159, 164
Pinot Meunier 21, 128
Pinot Nero 129
Pinot Noir 21, 24, 25, 26-30,
    31, 66, 113, 126, 128, 129, 139,
    155, 158, 160, 166
Pinotage 24, 46, 62, 68
pizza 161
Plavac Mali 65, 134
Ponce, Bodegas y Viñedos 53
Ponzi 107
Port 68, 87, 115, 116, 118, 149
Pošip 145
Pouilly-Fumé 82
Poulsard 124
poultry 136-7, 161
Prager, Weingut 102
prestige cuvées 128

Primitivo 56, 62
Prion, Dom. de 64
Prophet's Rock 102, 107
Prosecco 87, 115, 126, 161
pudding wine *see* sweet wine

QR codes 11
quality hierarchies 11, 26, 64,

Rabigato 118
Recioto della Valpolicella 125
red wine 64
  Argentinian 60
  Australian 10, 34, 38, 44,
    49, 60
  Austrian 10, 65
  Bulgarian 30
  Chilean 10, 29, 31, 34, 40,
    44, 60, 62
  chilling 29, 31
  Chinese 38, 40
  Croatian 65
  English 166
  food with 24, 28, 158, 159,
    160, 166, 169
  French 9, 26, 30, 32, 36, 38,
    42, 46, 48, 58, 64
  German 11, 29, 30, 125
  Greek 65
  Hungarian 30
  Israeli 46, 49
  Italian 9, 29, 40, 44, 49,
    54–7, 159, 169
  Lebanese 160
  Moroccan 46, 160
  New Zealand 10, 29–30, 34,
    160
  Portuguese 10, 52, 65
  Romanian 30
  South African 34, 46, 62
  Spanish 9, 11, 40, 44, 49,
    50–3
  sparkling 129, 154
  sweet 31
  Swiss 64
  Uruguayan 64–5
  USA 29, 38, 44, 49, 60, 62
Reserva 11
Rex Hill 107
Ribolla Gialla 9, 108, 144, 154,
  163
rice, pulses and grains 151

Ridgeview 129
Riedel, Claus 18
Riesling 11, 70, 71, 100–3, 104,
  100, 122, 125, 155, 156, 158,
  159, 160, 161
Rijk's 62
Rioja 41, 49, 50, 52, 71, 110, 112
Rippon 30
Riserva 11
Rivesaltes 120
Rolle *see* Vermentino
Romania 30
Rondinella 57, 125
rosado 69
rosato 68
rosé 66–9
  Argentinian 68
  Australian 68
  Chilean 68
  dry 144, 145, 156, 159
  food with 25, 69, 142, 164,
    169
  French 66
  Italian 68, 69, 169
  New Zealand 68
  Portuguese 68
  South African 68
  Spanish 68
  sparkling 26, 69, 128, 139
  sweet 68
  USA 68–9
  see also pink wine
Rosso di Montepulciano 161
Roussanne 48, 135, 150
Ruby Port 118
Rutherglen Muscat 99, 115,
  120
Rutherglen Topaque 94

saignée 26, 66
Sainte Lucie, Dom. 66
Samos 99, 120
Sancerre 82
Sangiovese 24, 54, 57, 159
Sassicaia 40, 57
Satèn 78, 129
sauces 152–4
Sauternes 84, 92, 94, 115,
  122, 164
Sauvignon Blanc 36, 71, 75,
  82–6, 87, 92, 104, 122, 124,
  129, 140, 142, 155, 156, 161

Savagnin 124
Schléret, Charles 99
Seifried 107
Sélection de Grains Nobles
  99, 102, 115, 124
Semillon 71, 82, 84, 92–5,
  122, 124, 155, 156
Seppelt 129
Sequillo 91
Seresin 30, 84
serving wine 16–17, 20
  temperature 14, 15, 31
shellfish 139, 142
Sherry 115, 119–20, 121, 156,
  161, 170
Shiraz *see* Syrah/Shiraz
Sideways (film) 42
Single Quinta Port 118
smells
  red wine 27, 33, 37, 43, 59
  white wine 73, 77, 83, 89,
    93, 97, 101, 105
Smith, Charles 102
Soave 143, 154
South Africa
  Durbanville 86, 163
  Elgin 86
  Stellenbosch 34, 62
  Swartland 34, 91
Spain
  Alentejo 68
  Andalucía 119
  Bierzo 9, 53
  Catalonia 49, 52, 113
  Cigales 53
  Manchuela 53
  Monterrei 53
  Navarra 49, 52, 68
  Priorat 49
  Rías Baixas 110
  Ribeira Sacra 53
  Ribera del Duero 52–3
  Rioja 49, 50, 52, 110, 112
  Rueda 9, 110
  Txakoli 112
  Utiel Requena 53
  Valdeorras 9, 53, 110
  Valdepeñas 52
  Valencia 53
  Vinho Verde 68
sparkling wine 126–9
  Australian 80, 129

Brazilian 129
English 69, 78, 115, 126, 129,
  145, 161, 166
food with 115, 145, 156, 158,
  159, 166
French 66, 78, 128
Italian 78, 99, 154
opening 16
pink 26, 69, 128
red 31, 129, 154
South African 129
Spanish 78
sparkling Shiraz 31, 129
USA 129
Spätburgunder *see* Pinot
  Noir
Spätlese 11, 125, 160
spicy foods 156–60
Spy Valley 102
Stanton & Killeen 94
Steen 91
sticky wine *see* sweet wine
store-cupboard jars 155
storing wine 14
straw wine 115, 122, 125
Strohwein 125
Suduiraut, Ch. 122
Super Tuscans 40, 56–7
surf 'n' turf 139
sweet wine 86, 96, 122–5
  Austrian 125
  food with 115, 170
  French 99, 122, 124
  German 125
  Greek 96, 99, 120
  Hungarian 124
  Italian 124–5
  red wine 31
  rosé 68
  Spanish 170
sweetness scales 11, 100
Switzerland 64
symbols, key to 6
Syrah/Shiraz 9, 10, 24, 25, 31,
  32–5, 38, 46, 48, 49, 66,
  68, 72, 75, 87, 115, 129, 159

takeout foods 161
Tannat 24, 58, 64–5
tannins 31, 36, 41, 46, 56, 120
Tawny Port 118, 149
Te Whare Ra 102

temperature 14, 15, 31
Tempranillo 10, 24, 49, 50, 52
Thévenet, Jean-Paul 64
Tignanello 57
Tinta Barroca 116
Tinta Cão 65, 116
Tinta del País 52, 53
Tinta Roriz 10, 52, 116
Tinta de Toro 52
Tinto Fino 52
Tokaji 115, 124
Torres 53
Torrontés 71, 140
Touriga Franca 65, 116
Touriga Nacional 10, 24, 25, 65, 68, 116
Trebbiano Toscana 124
Triebaumer 65
Trimbach 102
Trinity Hill 34
Trockenbeerenauslese 11, 115, 125
Trousseau 124
Truchard 80
Txomín Etxaníz, 112
Tyrell's 94

Umathum 65
Undurraga 86
Universal glass 18
Uruguay 64–5
USA

California 29, 38, 44, 60, 62, 68–9, 75, 80, 91, 102, 129
New York State 102
Oregon 29, 107
Washington State 38, 44, 60, 80, 102, 107
Vajra 99
Valdivieso 40
Vale Maria, Quinta do 65
Valpolicella Ripasso 125
varietal wines 10, 42, 58
Vasse Felix 80
Vega Sicilia 53
vegetables 146-50
Vendange Tardive 99, 102, 115, 122
Verdejo 9, 70, 110
Verdicchio 108, 154
Vermentino 108, 154
Villiera 129
Vin doux naturel 98, 99, 120
vin jaune 162
Vin de Paille 115, 124
Vin Santo 115, 124
Viña Falernia 34
Viña Leyda 29
Viña Mar 29
Viña von Siebenthal 40
vintage wines 118, 128, 139
Viognier 32, 34, 71, 72–5
Visintini 84, 107

Viura 71, 110, 112, 113
Vouvray 115, 124

Wachter-Wiesler 65
Weinbach, Dom. 102, 107
White Merlot 68
White Port 118
white wine 76
  Australian 75, 80, 86, 92, 94, 102, 155
  Austrian 102
  Chilean 10, 68, 86
  Croatian 145
  English 146, 166
  food with 70–1, 160, 166, 169, 170
  French 9, 48, 72, 76, 82, 84, 88, 92, 99, 102, 104, 107
  German 100
  Greek 96
  Italian 9, 84, 96, 106, 107, 108–9, 143, 169
  New Zealand 10, 75, 80, 82, 84, 91, 102, 107
  Portuguese 10, 96
  South African 75, 86, 91
  Spanish 9, 78, 96, 110–13, 142, 170
  USA 75, 80, 84, 91, 102, 107
White Zinfandel 68, 69
Wiemer, Hermann J. 102
wine cabinets and chillers 14

Wine & Soul 65
wood see oak
Woodward Canyon 38, 80

Xarello 113

Yabby Lake 80
Yalumba 75
Yquem, Ch. d' 122

Zalto 18
Zero Dosage 128
Zinfandel 24, 25, 62, 159
Zinfandel Blush 68, 69
Zweigelt 31, 65

acknowledgments

A huge, gigantic, colossal thanks to all these wonderful people, all of whom have helped more than they probably know (and some of whom will sadly never know): Mum and Dad, Jane Carr, Johnny Ray, Anne Kibel, Amelia and Matthew Jukes, Elizabeth Ferguson, Will Drew, Jancis Robinson, Michael Cox, Fiona Beckett, Charlotte Hey, Mary Rochester Gearing, Helen Chesshire, Hannah Tovey, Chris, Anne and Philip Parkinson, Astrid Lewis, Simon McMurtrie, Graham Holter, Patrick Schmitt, Patrick Sandeman, Andy Clarke, Bruno Cernecca, Hugh Johnson, Charles Metcalfe, Janan Ganesh, Anne Scott, Robert Joseph, Gary Simons, Stefan Chomka, Ewan Lacey, Kathrin Leaver, Amy Grier, James Winter, Lisa Smosarski, Steve Grimley, Gary Werner, the rest of The Wine Gang – Tom Cannavan, Joanna Simon, Anthony Rose and David Williams, everyone at Ryland Peters & Small, including Manisha Patel and especially Stephanie Milner, and finally, my university tutor who told me to do my dissertation on wine.